CASHING IN YOUR CHIPS
HOW TO PROFITABLY SELL YOUR BUSINESS

CASHING IN
YOUR CHIPS
HOW TO PROFITABLY
SELL YOUR BUSINESS

Charles R Ryan

Dow Jones-Irwin
Homewood, Illinois 60430

Sponsoring editor: Jim Childs
Project editor: Jean Roberts
Production manager: Bette Ittersagen
Jacket design: Image House
Compositor: Publication Services, Inc.
Typeface: 11/13 Century Schoolbook
Printer: R. R. Donnelley & Sons Company

Library of Congress Cataloging-in-Publication Data

Ryan, Charles R.
    Cashing in your chips : how to profitably sell your business / Charles R. Ryan.
      p.   cm.
    Includes index.
    ISBN 0-87094-974-8
    1. Business enterprises, Sale of—United States. 2. Small business—United States—Valuation. I. Title.
    HD1393.25.R94   1989
    658.1'6—dc20   89–31518
                                        CIP

Printed in the United States of America

1 2 3 4 5 6 7 8 9 DO 6 5 4 3 2 1 0 9

*This book is dedicated to my clients,
from whom I have learned so much
while making a living and having fun*

INTRODUCTION

Every day in the United States people start new businesses Their motivations for becoming entrepreneurs vary widely, but virtually all of them want at least to earn a good living from their business and eventually create a financial asset that they can either pass on to their families or sell. Some businesses last only a few weeks, others several years, a few for a lifetime. Fewer still, probably no more than about 25 percent, will survive into another generation of ownership in the same family. But no matter how many years a business survives, there is little certainty that it will be a financial success when all is said and done.

Recently I met a business owner who had started his company more than 40 years earlier. He was proud that his company had never lost money in the sense that the revenue collected each year was always more than direct business expenses. The owner felt that over the years he had taken out a good salary that allowed him to pay for his house and apparently fund most of his retirement. The owner's son learned the details of the business from the ground up and moved into management.

But as the industry changed, the business owner kept running things the same way, using the same old equipment. Eventually the company stopped growing because it was less competitive. By then the owner had run out of new ideas. Because the son had never worked anywhere else or obtained a broader education, he lacked understanding of the management principles he needed to succeed under the new industry conditions. After the company's sales stopped growing, they actually started to decline.

Eventually the father retired, partly because the company couldn't support both him and his son, much less make a return on the money he had invested in his business. When the son eventually proved unable to keep the business going, there were few alternatives. By then the business had little value as a going concern. It had good accounts receivable and no debts, but the old machinery and equipment, although worth more than their depreciated value, weren't worth a lot. Also, no one in the company had kept up with changes in the tax laws, so the owner had to pay a lot more income tax on the liquidation of his assets than he would have had to pay if he had carried out his plans earlier. By the end of this business owner's career, he had little financial success to show for his efforts and no legacy for his family. It didn't have to turn out that way.

First as a business advisory officer in a major bank and now as an independent adviser to business owners and their families, I have helped entrepreneurs improve the return on their investments in private businesses and professional practices. I have also helped owners devise and carry out ownership transition plans for their closely held businesses. I have seen business owners and their families operate a company for years, sometimes decades, without giving any serious thought to whether they are making an adequate return on their investment of time and money. Often they have not even realistically considered whether they can eventually transfer their businesses profitably to new owners, either in their family or outside of it.

I realize, and polls of business owners invariably point out, that people start or own businesses for many valid reasons in addition to making a return on a financial investment. People may have an intrinsic interest in a skill or technology, they may want to feel independent, or they may simply never have experienced any other kind of employment. As an adviser I frequently have to point out to business owners that they are not making enough of a return on their investment to justify their financial risk and effort. Often they quickly respond that they aren't just running their business for the money or that they operate their business in order to minimize taxes. Yet almost without fail, and especially as they get older, business owners start to talk about getting returns on their investments when they want to justify the selling price of their businesses. And unless they are using questionable tax practices, business owners, even with careful professional planning, usually pay considerable income taxes in some form if they are truly financially successful. Finally, I have seen owners who have run a company for 30 years or more decide, on an apparent whim or as the result of sudden illness or death, to sell their life's work in a matter of days without assistance from any qualified professionals who have been through such a process before. Seldom is the result ideal.

Typically when business school classes or books for entrepreneurs discuss the eventual sale of a successful business, they talk about public stock offerings. Companies that can go public have usually developed highly successful business concepts that need access to the huge pool of public investment funds if they are to expand to their full potential. Realistically speaking, extremely few private companies will ever go public.

This book is addressed to the owners of the hundreds of thousands of relatively small independent businesses that compose the backbone of many segments of our economy. Although many of these businesses may be successful, they will never grow to giant proportions or go public. Because their companies aren't candidates for public stock offerings, most private business owners have to come up with some other sort of exit strategy if they want to eventually make a return on their investment and recoup their cash.

Part of the appeal of business ownership to many people is that it is something of a game, a game in which the score is kept with money. As in the game of poker, business owners who are successful will be able to cash in their chips when it comes time to finish playing and give up day-to-day involvement in the company they have created, purchased, or inherited.

This book is about measuring, planning, managing, and controlling the process of cashing in your chips and exiting a business successfully. Although in many cases the process will involve eventually selling the business, more issues are involved than just putting the company on the market one day and hoping for a high price. In some cases owners want to exit a business without selling it per se. Or a particular business may not be salable. Therefore, the overall process is much broader than just planning to sell a business.

Owners of the hundreds of thousands of private companies and professional practices in the United States have a cumulative investment of many billions of dollars tied up in their businesses. In most cases those businesses are their most valuable financial assets. Yet most owners typically devote very little time and expertise to managing the rate of return and eventual ownership transition of their own businesses. If, as a consultant and fiduciary adviser, I did as little, I would be at least severely criticized and possibly sued for negligence.

The purpose of this book is to give business owners a more comprehensive view of the factors that make their businesses profitable or unprofitable. In particular, it stresses the importance of return on investment, ownership transition, and exit strategy. The ideas and examples provided throughout the book offer a framework for addressing these issues. The book is also intended to make people think about the range of options, or in some cases lack of options, they may have for cashing in their chips. I hope this information will help business owners and their families receive the greatest possible value from their private business investments.

The first chapters—Developing an Exit Strategy, Your Business Life Cycle, Has Your Business Really Ever Made Any Money? and Questions of Value—are intended to help you think through or rethink the basic assumptions of your business. This information should help you decide whether your business is really financially successful and why it may or may not be as valuable as you want it to be. These chapters will help you determine whether your business is now making, or is likely to make in the future, the return on investment that you should expect.

The next set of chapters—Setting Meaningful Business Objectives, Preparing to Cash In Your Chips, Creating a Dynasty, and Selling: The Ultimate Transition Option—discuss ideas for withdrawing your investment from your business and carrying out a management or ownership transition. Some business owners will be able to use any or all the investment extraction and transition routes described. In other cases, either by your choice as an owner or by circumstance, only one potential transition strategy may apply to your business.

When you receive advice on achieving a better financial return and managing ownership transition in your business you need to consider the perspective of the adviser. An attorney tends to see business transition and exit strategy issues as primarily legal questions. CPAs tend to see them as tax issues. Bankers will naturally be most aware of the effect on the company's financial structure. These professions are a typical business owner's most common advisers. Each of their perspectives is important and potentially valuable. But for your business to provide you with its maximum potential reward, be sure you are taking the broadest possible view. Although you need to carefully consider legal, tax, and banking concerns, you also need to look at them in the context of general business and investment management.

In successful businesses income taxes are a major expense. Tax effects are relevant to both operations and ownership transition planning. The tax codes are complex, change constantly, and vary in their importance with particular situations. Some examples in this book ignore tax considerations because they are not relevant to the point being made. That is, taxes are simply a given that you'll have to deal with no matter what course of action you select. You need to remember that if the figures are calculated on a pretax basis, as a business owner you will ultimately have to pay taxes. In other examples the approximate tax effects for different business options are estimated because the options will have fundamentally different tax impacts. In these cases the tax effects calculated are only approximate and are used simply to illustrate a point or alert you to a possible issue for further consideration. Tax laws and their application in practice are almost always in flux. You need to use the services of experienced, up-to-date tax professionals before undertaking any major business planning or business transaction actions. The information in this book should never be considered a substitute for professional tax or legal services.

Your ultimate benefit from this book may not be the specific ideas, strategies, and methods that I explain. The longest-lasting and most important benefit may be that it stimulates your thinking and helps you look at return on investment and transition issues either for the first time or in a new light. I think it is important for you to give disciplined and systematic consideration to maximizing the financial rewards from your business well before the time comes to retire or sell. I hope my thoughts assist in that process.

Charles R. Ryan

CONTENTS

CASHING IN YOUR CHIPS
YOUR CHIPS
HOW TO PROFITABLY
SELL YOUR BUSINESS

CHAPTER 1

DEVELOPING AN
EXIT STRATEGY

When Tenzing Norgay, who along with Edmund Hillary was the first to climb Mt. Everest, was asked what he thought about on the mountain's summit, he answered, "How to get down." Just as successful mountain climbers who take risks are always thinking about how they will get down from the mountain, business owners have to keep asking themselves how they are eventually going to cash in their chips and achieve a financial return for their risks and sacrifices.

WHAT MOST BUSINESS PLANNING
BOOKS NEVER MENTION

Every year thousands of people start new businesses or make major investments in existing businesses. To do so they take whatever money they have saved or can borrow from relatives, friends, associates, investors, or banks and put it into the risky and illiquid asset called a closely held business. Would-be entrepreneurs can draw on a vast reservoir of books, articles, and classes to learn such things as business planning, marketing, and personnel management. Entrepreneurs are driven to use their human and financial capital to grow a successful business. The initial planning and dreaming phase centers on spending money, producing goods or services, and making sales.

As owners make investments and accumulate earnings in their companies, they need to think about how they will eventually retrieve the assets they have invested. Owners should avoid committing funds to a business if they haven't established a means of withdrawing those funds in the future. An *exit strategy* is a plan for retrieving invested funds from a closely held business.

Many business builders will initially fail and thus suffer an undesired exit strategy. But many will initially succeed. The ancient Greeks are said not to have considered people successful until they had died with dignity. Likewise, business owners cannot be judged successful until they have profitably passed ownership of their assets to someone else or otherwise cashed in their chips. All things come to an end, and, if only due to the natural life span of its founder, the ownership and operation of a business must eventually pass from the current owner's control.

A business investment is more than the cash that the owner initially puts into the company. It also includes the profits or increase in asset values that accumulate in a successful enterprise. Just as some people are said to be "house poor" when they own a valuable residence but have no money available to put into other investments or to use for leisure, many entrepreneurs become "business poor" when they own a company or professional practice that generates a satisfactory living but nothing more. Their net worth becomes tied up in a risky, illiquid asset that may or may not yield a satisfactory rate of return.

A complete business plan needs a viable exit strategy from the start. Such a strategy considers questions that apply not only to starting or buying a business but also to expanding an already successful business.

How Large an Investment Will Be Made in the Business?

When evaluating an investment, business owners should measure not only any initial cash contribution but also the value of any labor or property they contribute. They should also consider the cost of *not* putting their money into an alternative investment.

How Much Money Is the Business Expected to Earn?

As a business owner, you must be realistic about the amount of money a particular business or business expansion is likely to earn. We have all read stories in the business press about owners who become wealthy from minuscule initial investments. But many entrepreneurs who have been in business for years barely recover their initial investments. In most cases competitive pressure and operational realities limit the probable earnings of a given business to a range of industry norms.

The computer software industry, for example, has a reputation for creating fantastic earnings. One small software company I know of has struggled for years to perfect and market its product. The owners have put in all their money and thousands of days of their lives. Yet their financial returns to date are limited to salaries about equal to what they would make working for someone else. What keeps these people going is a financial goal they have worked out on a computer spreadsheet that says all of them will be millionaires as soon as the company's annual sales volume reaches a certain point. The problem is that their financial projections assume net profit margins of about 40 percent. But as companies like theirs grow, overhead expenses increase. In fact, industry data indicate that software companies of the size they plan to become have average profit margins of less than 15 percent. These people are likely to be disappointed because their financial expectations are unrealistic.

When Will the Money Be Made?

As a business owner you have to establish a time horizon for your investments. If you plan to retire in five years, then you must be able to recover your investment, one way or the other, within that time. But you can't expect to make an equal amount of profit every year. In most businesses, you should anticipate an unprofitable start-up period, and you must factor this in to any realistic estimate of your company's lifetime earnings.

Many business owners let start-up losses get out of control in the mistaken belief that their investment will be returned later. In one situation a business owner purchased a new business for $750,000, which might have been reasonable had it been a mature operation. But in this case the company needed to grow considerably to become profitable, and it therefore experienced $400,000 in losses over a four-year period before reaching break-even, making the buyer's total investment $1,150,000. Since the potential annual profit for this business is only about $115,000, the owner can expect to earn just a 10 percent rate of return from the total funds invested in the business, which is not very high. You need to appreciate the effect a delay in business earnings will have on your total investment. If the delay is too long, your investment might grow so large that your business will never be able to give you a return on it.

In What Form Will You Get a Return on Your Investment?

Some businesses generate positive cash flow that can be distributed to the owners from day-to-day operations. Others return their owners' investment by increasing the value of assets owned by the business or the market value of the business itself.

Even if your company is profitable from an accounting standpoint, you may not be able to take out as much money as you would like. Some businesses require continuous reinvestment in order to remain competitive. This is especially true in industries with frequent technological changes or severe competition. In such a business, all the profits may remain tied up in the company.

What Form of Business Ownership Is Appropriate?

The basic forms of ownership—sole proprietorship, partnership, and corporation—stay the same. But as your business and its environment change, you may need to reconsider the best form of ownership. Even though a certain form of ownership may make sense for as long as you want to stay involved in the business, it may work against you when it comes time to cash in some of your earnings or provide for ownership transition.

To create and manage an exit strategy, you must be aware of the amount and trend of your investment in the business. Standard accounting reports don't automatically provide this information, but the data should be available within the accounting records. You will need to create your own reports as part of a business plan to control and track an exit strategy. Maintaining the information will not be difficult once you've developed the initial concept. This chapter will discuss the concepts, and the third chapter, Has Your Business Really Ever Made Any Money?, will illustrate the principles with financial case studies.

HOW MUCH IS INVESTED?

Are you really aware of how much money you have invested in your company? To get your business started you may have taken a specific amount of money out of your savings, inheritance, or other investments. Or you may have contributed certain equipment or other assets that were needed for operations. These are all easily recognizable investments, but in most cases your entire initial investment involves much more than you might expect.

Few people stop to consider that the money or other assets they put into their businesses cannot be earning money elsewhere. Any profit you forgo in this way is called an *opportunity cost*. For example, assume that the money you put into your business would be able to earn an average of 10 percent in other investments. If you make only an 8 percent return on your business investment, you have incurred an opportunity cost of 2 percent. Therefore, during any time period in which you have funds tied up in a closely held company, you have to give up the opportunity to earn money from an alternative investment.

You incur a second opportunity cost if you or your family members give up other income to spend time developing your business. For example, you may be able to earn $35,000 a year working for someone else. If you choose instead to develop your own business and it does not make enough money to pay you a $35,000 salary, then your investment will include the difference between $35,000 and the amount the business actually pays you. This cost will continue to accrue until your own business can pay you more than the $35,000 you might earn elsewhere.

And if any of your relatives work for the company at a lower wage than they could earn elsewhere, the difference between their earnings from your business and their forgone salary constitutes an additional investment.

Tax savings may partially offset your initial investment. Many times the start-up losses from a new business can be used to reduce income tax that would otherwise have been paid on another family member's salary or other sources of income. Such a tax savings will reduce the amount of money you have invested. Uncle Sam is, in effect, subsidizing your business. For example, assume that your business loses $10,000 in the first year and your family has other taxable income of $35,000. If you are in the 28 percent income tax bracket, then the income tax you would otherwise have paid will be reduced by $10,000 × 28 percent, or $2,800.

CALCULATING THE INITIAL INVESTMENT

Tables 1–1 through 1–4 calculate the amount of money an entrepreneur can expect to invest in a start-up business during the first five years of its operation. The total investment is measured in terms of both the initial cash contribution and the opportunity cost of forgoing income from other employment and alternative investments. These tables make several initial assumptions about the entrepreneur's situation:

1. A total of $100,000 in cash and other assets are available for investment.
2. The cash and other assets could earn an average return of 10 percent annually if they were invested in something other than the start-up business. For example, the funds might be kept in a mixed portfolio of stocks, bonds, and bank certificates.
3. The entrepreneur could earn $35,000 per year if employed for someone else, and the entrepreneur's spouse could earn $25,000.
4. The entrepreneur needs $35,000 after taxes annually for living expenses and has $10,000 per year in personal tax deductions.

TABLE 1–1
Personal Income without Business

	Year 0	Year 1	Year 2	Year 3	Year 4	Year 5
Beginning cash and other assets	$100,000	$100,000	$117,568	$136,400	$156,588	$178,230
Salary earnings capability:						
Entrepreneur		35,000	35,000	35,000	35,000	35,000
Spouse		25,000	25,000	25,000	25,000	25,000
Earnings on cash and other assets		10,000	11,757	13,640	15,659	17,823
Income taxes and FICA		(17,433)	(17,924)	(18,452)	(19,017)	(19,623)
After-tax income		52,568	53,832	55,188	56,642	58,200
Annual living expenses		35,000	35,000	35,000	35,000	35,000
Discretionary income		17,568	18,832	20,188	21,642	23,200
Cash invested in business	–0–					
Ending cash and other assets	$100,000	$117,568	$136,400	$156,588	$178,230	$201,430

TABLE 1–2
Far West Manufacturing Business Plan

	Year 0	Year 1	Year 2	Year 3	Year 4	Year 5
Annual sales		$200,000	$300,000	$420,000	$550,000	$700,000
Gross profit margin		40.0%	40.0%	40.0%	40.0%	40.0%
General, sales, and administration costs		$ 90,000	$110,000	$130,000	$155,000	$190,000
Sales/assets		3.0	3.0	3.0	3.0	3.0
		Income Statement				
Annual income before owner/manager salary		$ (10,000)	$ 10,000	$ 38,000	$ 65,000	$ 90,000
Owner/manager salary		0	0	15,000	25,000	35,000
Interest expense on business liabilities		1,852	4,738	7,413	9,122	10,324
Pretax income		(11,852)	5,262	15,587	30,878	44,676
Corporate income tax		0	789	2,338	4,632	6,701
Net income		$ (11,852)	$ 4,473	$ 13,249	$ 26,247	$ 37,974
		Balance Sheet				
Assets	$60,000	$ 66,667	$100,000	$140,000	$183,333	$233,333
Liabilities	0	18,519	47,379	74,130	91,217	103,243
Net worth	$60,000	$ 48,148	$ 52,621	$ 65,870	$ 92,116	$130,090

TABLE 1–3
Personal Income with Business

	Year 0	Year 1	Year 2	Year 3	Year 4	Year 5
Beginning cash and other assets	$100,000	$40,000	$31,233	$18,524	$17,844	$23,546
Salary earnings capability:						
Entrepreneur		25,000	0	15,000	25,000	35,000
Spouse			25,000	25,000	25,000	25,000
Earnings on cash and other assets		4,000	3,123	1,852	1,784	2,355
Income taxes and FICA		(2,767)	(5,832)	(7,533)	(11,083)	(14,633)
After-tax income		26,233	22,291	34,320	40,702	47,722
Annual living expenses		35,000	35,000	35,000	35,000	35,000
Discretionary income		(8,767)	(12,709)	(680)	5,702	12,722
Cash invested in business	60,000					
Ending cash and other assets	$ 40,000	$31,233	$18,524	$17,844	$23,546	$36,268

TABLE 1–4
Summary of Total Investment

	Year 0	Year 1	Year 2	Year 3	Year 4	Year 5
Initial cash investment	$(60,000)					
Discretionary income with business minus discretionary income without business		$(26,335)	$ (31,541)	$ (20,868)	$ (15,940)	$ (10,478)
Total investment in business	(60,000)	(26,335)	(31,541)	(20,868)	(15,940)	(10,478)
Cumulative business investment	$(60,000)	$(86,335)	$(117,876)	$(138,744)	$(154,684)	$(165,162)

Beginning with year 0, the date the business would begin, Table 1–1 calculates how much the entrepreneur's family could earn and reinvest over five years *without* starting a new business. Earnings come from the two salaries and from return on investment from the $100,000. After paying taxes and living expenses, the family is assumed to invest all its discretionary income in other assets that will continue to earn 10 percent annually. By the end of the fifth year the entrepreneur could accumulate $201,430 in cash and other assets by saving all discretionary income and continuing to make alternative investments.

The entrepreneur's business operations for the first five years are summarized in Table 1–2. The $60,000 initially needed to fund operations comes out of the entrepreneur's original $100,000 in cash and other assets. During the first year the business loses $10,000. The entrepreneur finances this loss by not taking any salary and by incurring $18,519 in liabilities such as accounts payable or a bank credit line. In the second year the business makes a small amount of money, but again the entrepreneur reinvests the earnings instead of taking a salary. As the business grows in the third year and becomes increasingly profitable, the entrepreneur starts taking a salary. By the fifth year there are enough earnings to pay a $35,000 annual salary, which is the amount of money the entrepreneur could make working for someone else, and even after interest and taxes the business is earning $37,974. Throughout this period the entrepreneur has used all earnings over and above salaries and corporate taxes to pay for growth and reduce the company's dependence on debt.

At this point some people might conclude that the entrepreneur has taken a $60,000 investment and created a business that earns almost $40,000 per year after paying a $35,000 salary to its owner. But that conclusion ignores the entrepreneur's opportunity cost. Table 1–3 calculates the entrepreneur's personal income while owning the business in the same manner as Table 1–1 calculates her or his income without the business. In years 1 and 2 the entrepreneur has no salary, and in years 3 and 4 the salary is less than could be earned working for someone else. The spouse's salary from other employment remains the same as before, but earnings from cash and other assets are substantially reduced because less money is available for alternative investments. Income tax and FICA (Social Security) payments are lower because less money is earned. Taxes are especially low in year 1 when the entrepreneur is assumed to have set up the business so as to use the $10,000 business loss to offset the spouse's salary and other income. Since living expenses exceed after-tax income in years 1 through 3, the entrepreneur dips into cash and other assets, further reducing earnings from those sources.

Bringing together all this information, Table 1–4 calculates the entrepreneur's total investment in the business. This investment includes not only the $60,000 put into the business during the start-up phase, but also the discretionary income sacrificed during the five years of the company's operation. The total of the initial cash contribution and the five years of reduced discretionary income is $165,162. The same result can be calculated by comparing the $201,430 of cash and other assets available at the end of year 5 in Table 1–1 with the $36,268 in cash and other assets available at the end of year 5 in Table 1–3.

In this situation the owner's investment in this company is at least $165,000, or almost three times as much as the original $60,000 cash infusion made in year 0.

Additionally the company has accumulated about $70,000 in equity in its assets as measured by the increase in net worth from $60,000 to $130,091 during year 0 through year 5. In other words, the owner has tied up about $235,000 in this small company: the $165,000 outside investment plus the $70,000 in retained earnings that have been accumulated but not distributed to the owner.

Just to *break even* after five years of hard work in this business, the owner would have to sell the business for an amount sufficient to net $165,000 after taxes. Using methods that will be discussed in later chapters and assuming the most favorable possible terms of sale from the owner's viewpoint, this business would have to be sold for about $230,000 just to break even.

The actual amount invested in most private businesses is typically greater than the cash that people are aware of putting in. Even when people buy a company with no money down, the opportunity cost from forgone salary and lost income from alternative investments may still be a major investment.

If you are going to start or buy a business—or even if you already own one and want to understand your position better—it's useful to calculate your total investment. The information you gain can help put your exit strategy into perspective by describing the "nut you have to crack" before your business can break even. Only if your earnings exceed your total investment by the time you are through with active management can your company be considered a successful venture.

Managing Earnings Expectation

Of course, it is important to realistically measure the amount of money your business earns each year after the start-up period. The measurement techniques discussed in the previous section and the implications of their results will be covered in more detail in Chapters 2 and 3. But measurement after the fact is not enough. To be successful, you also need to know what kinds of goals to set and how to achieve them. In most situations it is not realistic to expect to recover all your money at once when you sell a business that has not been highly profitable. Only if you pay close attention to earnings, cash flow, and return on investment will you have a chance to earn and enjoy the rewards that you deserve *while* you are working in your company and reap the full benefits of your investment when the time comes to cash in your chips.

I find that managers of closely held businesses frequently set earnings expectations for their companies that are much too low. By not attempting to maximize earnings and cash flow each year, they forgo the chance to reinvest the funds elsewhere or just to enjoy the fruits of their efforts. And by not keeping their businesses in peak financial condition they will probably miss some opportunities forever. Weak cash flow and overall financial stability do not permit their businesses to take advantage of prospective acquisitions or other expansion opportunities.

It is possible, perhaps due to factors beyond your control, that the value of your business may eventually start to decline rather than increase. If you have not taken advantage of early opportunities to recover investment from your business in the form of annual earnings and cash flow, that money may be lost in the event of a decline of your firm's industry, location, or economic conditions.

WHEN WILL THE MONEY BE MADE?

For business owners money in hand today is worth more than money they will receive in the future. Funds that are no longer needed in the business for day-to-day operations can be reinvested elsewhere to compound and earn greater returns or can be used to reduce debt and interest expenses. If throughout its life a business generates a steady earnings stream that can be withdrawn from operations, then the owners are in fact carrying out an exit strategy during the daily course of running their company. By withdrawing money sooner rather than later business owners are recovering their initial investments plus earning a return on the accumulated profits of their firms.

In some cases the primary form of business earnings is from the appreciation of assets rather than income from day-to-day operations. To be sure you are making financial progress, you must carefully monitor the annual appreciation in property value to see if it is increasing enough to justify keeping it. I recently saw a corporation that was no longer able to earn reasonable income from ongoing operations but was being retained by its stockholders strictly because the property in which the business operated was worth 50 times its original cost. By any standards that is indeed a substantial increase. But the stockholders had not stopped to calculate that, over the many years they had owned the property, the average pretax rate of return was only about 6 percent annually, and in recent years the increase in property value was probably only keeping up with inflation. These business owners would have been much better

off had they sold their property several years earlier and reinvested the funds elsewhere.

PLAN CAREFULLY BEFORE REINVESTING
EACH YEAR'S EARNINGS

After the start-up phase a successful business should regularly
earn more money than the amount needed to pay the owner's
salary or support existing operations. If a business is growing,
needs to replace worn-out equipment, or has debts that should
be repaid to reduce financial risk, then it may make sense to
retain most of these excess earnings. Some people take more
money out of their business than prudent financial management
would advise. But I have noticed that many private business
owners make the error of habitually keeping all their businesses' earnings in the company even when this kind of investment
offers no growth opportunities.

There are several reasons for this. In the past, corporate tax
rates at all levels of income were lower than personal tax rates.
So if the owners left all the earnings in the corporation, they
would have more after-tax funds to invest even if the money
were simply put into a bank account or other investments unre-
lated to the business's main activity. And since the earnings
from these secondary investments within the corporation would
again be subject to lower tax rates, the money could compound
faster. The general strategy was eventually to cash in these
investments as part of the sale of the business at favorable capital gains rates when the owners decided to sell out.

Changes in the tax code since 1986 make the retention
of such unneeded assets in a corporation a potentially serious
financial mistake. First of all, capital gains taxes are no longer
being kept low. And for levels of taxable income above $75,000
the corporate income tax rates are higher than the personal
income tax rates (Table 1–5). But more damaging for people
who plan to sell their businesses is the end of the *General
Utilities Doctrine*. Under the prior tax code, when a corporation
sold its assets in the process of liquidating the business, the

TABLE 1–5
Effective Marginal Tax Rates

	Taxable Income					
	$25,000	*$50,000*	*$75,000*	*$100,000*	*$150,000*	*$335,000*
Personal (married)	15.0%	28.0%	33.0%	33.0%	28.0%	28.0%
Corporate	15.0	25.0	34.0	34.0	39.0	34.0

transaction could be structured so that the corporation itself owed no tax on the gain from the sale of its assets. Only the shareholders would be taxed. Now, in a sale of corporate assets, both the corporation *and* the shareholders may be liable for income taxes. This can result in double taxation of the increase in the value of the business's assets.

The effect of these changes in the tax code is that many business owners who thought they would receive relatively favorable tax treatment on the value of their business assets when it came time to sell them are in for a rude awakening. In my opinion a well-thought-out exit strategy will ensure that any earnings not needed for increased business growth or reduced financial risk are withdrawn from the business promptly in the most advantageous manner and reinvested in other assets.

Think Carefully before Putting Assets into a Corporation

One way to implement an effective exit strategy is to avoid putting too large an investment into the business in the first place. Owners of private companies typically take pride in how many thousands or millions of dollars of assets they have accumulated in their businesses. But managers of public companies that are under pressure to maximize returns to their shareholders typically take pride in how *few* corporate assets they need to conduct the business. They know that the key to maximizing shareholder value in most situations is to increase earnings and cash flow while using fewer assets.

As a business owner, then, you need to be careful not to tie up assets that your business doesn't need for ongoing operations. If your business is earning more money than it needs, be sure to take out these funds on a regular basis and reinvest them elsewhere.

It is not usually a good idea to lock up appreciating assets such as real estate in your business. First, unless the nature of your business is real estate ownership, your company can usually earn a superior rate of return by investing its money in more inventory or other operating assets on which the turnover is faster. And, if you retain appreciating assets in a corporation, you may be subject to double taxation. That is, you'll have to pay both corporate and personal income tax on the profit when you eventually sell the assets. Also, keeping unnecessary, valuable assets in the business may increase your overall risk in the event of business reversals or unfavorable, uninsured lawsuits

CONSIDER THE BEST FORM
OF BUSINESS OWNERSHIP

Traditionally almost all businesses of any size have been incorporated as standard corporations Among the advantages of this arrangement are

1. Limited financial liability of shareholders
2. Ease of transferring stock ownership.
3. More favorable possibilities for pension plans.
4. Lower income tax rates on earnings for small companies.

But today this conventional wisdom is sometimes ill-advised.

Over the years Congress has made access to pension and retirement benefit programs for noncorporate businesses relatively favorable. At the same time corporate income tax rates for many businesses have equaled or exceeded individual income tax rates. Since 1986 a number of corporations have found it to their shareholders' benefit to convert to some form of partnership or to "S" corporations, which are taxed like partnerships The main reason that traditional corpora tions may not be as good a means of asset ownership today, particularly for smaller companies, is the increased potential for double taxation when business assets are eventually sold.

To develop a successful exit strategy, you need to carefully consider whether your form of business ownership is correct for your current situation and future plans. Also, consider the possibility of dividing different business assets among more than one form of ownership. This is often a desirable strategy. The most typical case is where business owners create a partnership to own real estate that is then rented to an operating corporation owned by the same people.

SET TIME FRAMES

If you don't plan to operate your business indefinitely, have a time frame in mind for relinquishing ownership and management. Establishing this time horizon can help you make correct decisions regarding additional investments. As in the case of a personal residence, you may be unable to recover from a buyer the full value of any improvements you make to your business shortly before selling it. For example, a major investment in employee or management training may result in tremendous returns to the business over a period of several years. But it is unlikely to substantially increase the value of the business to a prospective investor who will take over the company in the next three months. On the other hand, owners who let their businesses decline due to lack of sufficient investment will probably pay a price for this when prospective buyers realize how much additional money and time they will need to put into the company to achieve its full profit potential.

Time frames for transferring business ownership will obviously be influenced by your age, health, and other objectives in life. Also, different types of businesses, like other things, go in and out of fashion depending on general perceptions about particular industries, regions, or the general economy. You need to acknowledge that your business might not be highly desirable to potential buyers forever. It may be better to sell a little too soon—before your product or region has peaked—than to wait too long and find that nobody wants what you have to offer at any reasonable price.

CHECKLIST FOR DEVISING
A BUSINESS EXIT STRATEGY

1. Calculate how much money you have invested, or will invest, in your business.
2. Estimate the amount and timing of earnings you can withdraw from the business during ongoing operations.
3. Verify that your form of business ownership is the most favorable for carrying out a profitable withdrawal of funds.
4. Establish a time horizon for implementing the strategy.
5. If the strategy involves selling your business, determine who will be the likely buyer and operate the business accordingly.
6. Have a specific plan for what to do with funds as you withdraw them from your business.

CHAPTER 2

YOUR BUSINESS LIFE CYCLE

Natural and human activities tend to progress through cycles, or phases, in which their basic characteristics change but eventually return to a prior condition. Cycles occur in climate, animal populations, designer fashions, stock markets, and national politics.

Businesses also tend to go through cycles as they develop. Periods of vigorous growth and expansion are typically followed by times of relative stability or even decline. Most business books and articles assume either that all businesses are currently in a growth cycle or that they should strive to be in one. This is because businesses that in the long run fail to meet the needs of expanding markets will be eclipsed by their rivals and will ultimately decline.

But this doesn't mean that the growth of a business is constant and inevitable. Foresighted business owners prepare for and deal with the inevitable plateaus of sales and earnings and keep a sharp lookout for the first signs of difficult going ahead.

Many events can slow, stop, or even reverse business growth:

1. Economic recession in the general economy.
2. Increased competitive pressure.
3. Saturation of a local market.
4. Changes in technology or consumer taste.

Despite the best efforts of management, many businesses simply run out of growth opportunities. These situations present a special challenge to owners who want to avoid a decline in the value and profitability of their businesses

As a business owner you need to develop a sense of where your business is in its life cycle and to understand the financial implications of its present and probable future position. The financial rewards you extract from your business will depend to a large extent on its position in the life cycle.

Every business or professional practice tends to go through the same general development phases. Each phase has different implications for effective management as well as cash flow to the owners. The basic phases are

1. Start-up
2. Expansion
3. Maturity
4. Decline

Even the largest companies go through the start-up phase at one point. The expansion period that leads to maturity can be very long for some businesses and quite short for others. When the decline phase lasts for a long enough period, even after years of successful profit, the firm's survival will be threatened. A decline eventually becomes difficult to turn around if it isn't checked. A period of growth following a period of maturity or decline, on the other hand, could signal the rejuvenation of the company. The following sections describe the conditions that characterize each of these phases and provide ideas that can help you cope with each

BUSINESS LIFE CYCLES FROM A CASH FLOW PERSPECTIVE

For investors who want to obtain cash from their businesses, the most important aspects of business life cycles are the cash flow characteristics associated with each phase. Figures 2–1 and 2–2 illustrate the general sales, earnings, and overall cumulative cash flow expected at various points in a classical business life cycle. Figure 2–1 illustrates the situation of a business that has begun to decline after its maturity. And Figure 2–2 shows the case of a business that is rejuvenating itself financially after a period of maturity and has begun to grow again

FIGURE 2–1

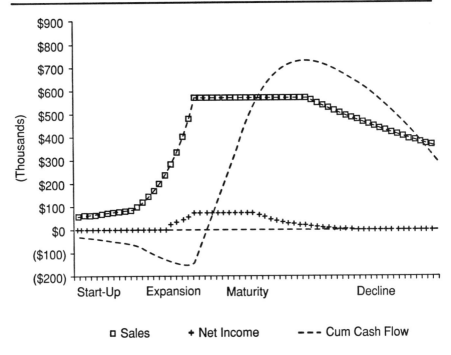

□ Sales   + Net Income   - - - Cum Cash Flow

FIGURE 2–2

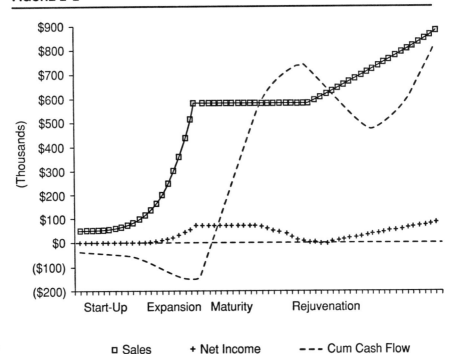

□ Sales   + Net Income   - - - Cum Cash Flow

In both situations sales begin at a low level during the start-up phase and do not produce sufficient revenue to cover all the operating expenses. Not only are the firms losing money from operations, but additional cash is used to finance assets and working capital. The result is a negative cash flow that accumulates over time. A business start-up phase can last an indefinite period of time. I have seen companies that still have start-up characteristics more than a decade after having begun operations. Frequently business owners cannot implement a viable marketing or operations strategy that will carry their businesses into the sustainable expansion phase that eventually leads to mature profitability.

If a business does establish a successful marketing strategy and supports it with efficient operations, then sales growth will accelerate into an expansion phase. As sales volume exceeds the break-even level, the business will become profitable from its current operations. But negative cash flows still frequently occur because more assets, accounts receivable, inventory, and equipment are needed to support the rapidly growing business volume. Even though the business may by this time be seen as a success, it may still be unable to provide its owners with excess cash they can take out and spend or invest elsewhere.

The maturity phase of a business occurs when sales growth levels off at a volume that produces more profit than needed to cover all expenses and asset replacement costs. This is the point at which the business becomes a *cash cow*. In this phase, large amounts of excess cash accumulate. Depending on the length of the phase, the owner might eventually be able to recover all the original investment and much more. If the maturity phase lasts indefinitely, the business becomes a kind of money machine. This can be particularly lucrative in businesses that have some kind of franchise in industries where business conditions do not change rapidly such as soft drink bottling, broadcasting, and some professional services.

But eventually even well-built machines wear out. Perhaps management isn't paying close attention, market conditions change, or competitors edge into a previously closed market. Without active reinvestment, and sometimes despite reinvestment, most businesses eventually experience a decline in either sales levels or profit margins. This decline phase is illustrated in the right-hand portion of Figure 2–1. After a period of maturity the cash cow stops giving milk as the firm stops generating more earnings than are needed to cover all operating and asset replacement costs. If the decline lasts long enough, the company will eventually be back where it started in terms of overall cash flow.

But there is an alternative to decline. Once a mature business starts to "wear out," its owners can make additional investments to rejuvenate it and propel it into another growth phase. In the short run such a rejuvenation phase, illustrated in the right-hand portion of Figure 2–2, creates negative cash flows for the same reasons that the initial expansion cycle does: money has to be invested in new facilities, promotional programs, and other parts of the operation. But if the rejuvenation is successful, the result should be growth to an even higher level of earnings and cash flow. The business will then be ready for a second phase of maturity and the attendant positive profit characteristics of a cash cow.

People ask me, "How long will my start-up phase last?" "How much time does it typically take to recover the money I originally invested in my business?" or "How much money can I afford to take out of my business?" There is no single correct answer to such questions. Business life-cycle phases last different lengths of time in different businesses. The length of the cycle is not particularly important. The important thing is to know which cycle you are currently in, and, if the characteristics of that cycle are not desirable, to take steps to move toward more favorable conditions that will eventually generate excess positive cash flow.

YOUR BUSINESS'S CURRENT LIFE-CYCLE PHASE

Several key business characteristics tend to define the business cycle. By applying a score to each key variable, you can determine what business life-cycle phase your company is in. The characteristics rated in Table 2–1 are

- Sales: both volume and growth rate.
- Earnings: levels of net income and cash flow.
- Financial condition: balance sheet strength.
- Customer and product base: diversification, growth.
- Operations: the smoothness of day-to-day activity.
- Information: does management know what's going on?

The level of development for each of these characteristics is assigned a number from zero through five, with the higher scores assigned to the more desirable conditions for each characteristic. Sample scores for each of the four basic business life-cycle phases are shown in Table 2–1.

A start-up with at least some sales and one or more customers scores only a 2. A growth company that is increasing sales rapidly but still not generating an overall positive cash flow might score around 18. Near the pinnacle a well-organized, mature business that is generating excess cash but not experiencing rapid sales growth achieves a score of 24. And a business that once had the excess positive cash flow characteristics of a mature company but now has a shrinking customer base and lower earnings is ranked 16.

As a practical matter few companies will be purely in one phase or another because the characteristics that indicate a business's position within the cycle do not inevitably change at the same rate. The scoring is weighted to put the most emphasis on sales growth, earnings in excess of the basic needs for survival, overall financial condition, and the nature of most companies' ultimate asset, its customer base.

The likely scores for companies in the various life-cycle phases tend to overlap as shown in Table 2–2. A well-organized growth company that still isn't producing a positive cash flow may score the same as a mature, profitable, but poorly organized company. A declining company may have the same overall score as a growth company, but the company's history and other facts not accounted for by the scores will show that this is an undesirable condition. Mature companies will tend, more than companies in other categories, to have well-organized operations and complete management information. But that is not always true; some otherwise mature companies are disorganized and produce regular earnings and positive

TABLE 2–1
Score Sheet to Determine Stage of Business Development

Points		Start-Up (Turnaround)	Growth (Rejuvenate)	Mature	Decline
	Sales				
1	Below break-even level	1			
5	Above break-even and growing faster than inflation and the overall economy		5		
3	Above break-even and growing only about as fast as inflation or the overall economy			3	
2	Lower than at a prior time period and not growing at the rate of inflation and the overall economy				2
	Earnings				
0	Less than needed to pay adequate salaries or all expenses, much less fund growth	0			
2	Able to pay adequate salaries and all expenses, but outside funds still needed to support growth or replace worn out/obsolete assets		2		2
5	More than enough to pay all expenses and meet capital needs; surplus cash is available to distribute to owners or fund additional investments			5	

TABLE 2–1—Continued

Points		Start-Up (Turnaround)	Growth (Rejuvenate)	Mature	Decline
	Financial Condition				
0	No working capital position, no retained earnings to finance assets	0			
2	Adequate working capital but insufficient retained earnings to finance growth or asset replacement		2		
5	Adequate working capital and enough retained earnings to finance growth or asset replacement internally			5	
3	Adequate overall capital but somewhat illiquid; tends to have worn out or obsolete fixed assets				3
	Customer or Product Base				
1	Dependent on a few customers/products for most sales	1			
5	Diversified customer/product base; new customers being added faster than old ones are lost		5		
3	Diversified customer/product base; enough new customers are attracted to replace those that are lost			3	
1	Customer/product base less diversified than in prior years, and old customers are lost faster than new ones are added				1

TABLE 2–1—Continued

Points		Start-Up (Turnaround)	Growth (Rejuvenate)	Mature	Decline
	Operations				
0	Few established procedures; key knowledge primarily in the head of owner or key employees	0			
2	Procedures are in place to regularize most operations and train new employees		2		
4	Day-to-day operations are smooth and efficient; loss of any single employee will not harm the firm			4	4
	Information Systems				
0	No reliable management reports to track key business variables, or reports are not timely	0			
2	Basic information available in a timely manner		2		
4	Complete information available to monitor and control all elements of the business			4	4
		2	18	24	16

TABLE 2–2
Typical Scores for Various Stages of Business Development

	1	2	3	4	5	6	7	8	9	10	11	12	13	14	15	16	17	18	19	20	21	22	23	24	25	26	27	28	29	30
Start-up (Turnaround)		*********************																												
Growth (Rejuvenate)					***																									
Mature														***																
Decline					***																									

cash flow without accurate information. But they will not be well-prepared for negative changes in their environment that threaten profitability. You can't simply look at a company's score and know for sure where it is in its cycle. But the process of evaluating your own company against these criteria will help determine the steps necessary to move toward a more desirable cash flow situation.

The life-cycle scores for nine actual businesses are shown in Table 2–3 as I ranked them at various stages of their development. Below each company's score is the number of years the firm had been in business as of the date I made this analysis.

START-UP

The primary characteristic of a start-up is a low volume of sales that does not produce cash flow sufficient to cover all the business's day-to-day operating expenses. The owners must therefore cover the losses by working for inadequate wages, living off their savings, or borrowing money. Negative cash flows are caused by both the operating losses and the need to have money invested in the assets used to operate the business. Typical start-ups are undercapitalized and therefore struggle from month to month to meet routine obligations. Sometimes a start-up company depends on a narrow customer base and constantly risks losing its revenue stream entirely. To top off their risks, start-ups often depend on the knowledge and ability of one person who keeps track of things by the "seat-of-the-pants" method.

Obviously start-ups are risky. They have a tremendous appetite for cash and depend heavily on one or a few customers and employees. A start-up may be surviving as long as it continues to make sales to at least one customer, but mere survival is not success to most people. According to the scoring method suggested in Table 2–1, any company that scores between 2 and 10 is probably either a start-up or a business that once progressed to a higher level but suffered financial reverses and is currently in danger of failing.

TABLE 2-3
Score Sheet to Determine Stage of Business Development

Points		Example Companies							
		A	B	C	D	E	F	G	H
	Sales								
1	Below break-even level	1		1					
5	Above break-even and growing faster than inflation and the overall economy				5	5	5		
3	Above break-even and growing only about as fast as inflation or the overall economy								3
2	Lower than at a prior time period and not growing at the rate of inflation and the overall economy		2					2	
	Earnings								
0	Less than needed to pay adequate salaries or all expenses, much less fund growth	0	0	0					
2	Able to pay adequate salaries and all expenses but outside funds still needed to support growth or replace worn out/obsolete assets				2			2	2
5	More than enough to pay all expenses and meet capital needs; surplus cash is available to distribute to owners or fund additional investments					5	5		

TABLE 2-3—Continued

Points		A	B	C	D	E	F	G	H
	Financial Condition								
0	Inadequate working capital position, no retained earnings to finance assets	0		0					
2	Adequate working capital but insufficient retained earnings to finance growth or asset replacement		2		2			2	2
5	Adequate working capital and enough retained earnings to finance growth or asset replacement internally					5	5		
3	Adequate overall capital but somewhat illiquid; tends to have worn out or obsolete fixed assets								
	Customer or Product Base								
1	Dependent on a few customers/products for most sales								
5	Diversified customer/product base; new customers being added faster than old ones are lost	5		5		5	5		
3	Diversified customer/product base; enough new customers are attracted to replace those that are lost				3				3
1	Customer/product base less diversified than in prior years, and old customers are lost faster than new ones are added		1					1	

Example Companies

TABLE 2-3—Continued

Points		Example Companies							
		A	B	C	D	E	F	G	H
	Operations								
0	Few established procedures; key knowledge primarily in the head of owner or key employees		0	0		0			
2	Procedures are in place to regularize most operations and train new employees	2					2	2	
4	Day-to-day operations are smooth and efficient; loss of any single employee will not harm the firm				4				4
	Information Systems								
0	No reliable management reports to track key business variables, or reports are not timely	0	0						
2	Basic information available in a timely manner			2	2	2		2	2
4	Complete information available to monitor and control all elements of the business						4		
	Total score	8	5	8	18	22	26	11	16
	Years in business	3	11	4	6	5	20	17	40

Table 2–3 shows that companies A and B have the characteristics of start-ups. Firm A has been in business only about
three years. Its sales are growing, but profit has still not caught
up with operating expenses. Despite negative cash flows that
must be financed by investors and borrowing, the company has
a positive outlook because the customer base is well-diversified
and growing. This firm appears to be poised to enter a profitable
expansion phase.

In contrast, company B has been operating for 11 years, and
it has never progressed beyond typical start-up characteristics.
In this case management failed to capitalize on early opportunities. Competitors thus had a chance to enter the market and take
away customers before company B had reached a solid break-even
sales volume. Although the owner eventually sold the business's
assets for nearly their original cost, company B was never able to
recover the years of lost opportunity cost that the owner incurred
during the time the business struggled to get off the ground.
By investing aggressively, new owners of company B were able to
push it into a growth phase in less than a year and to make rapid
progress toward true profitability.

GROWTH (REJUVENATION)

A company is in its growth phase when (1) it has brought its
sales level above break-even, (2) it can cover its day-to-day
operating expenses, and (3) it can pay reasonable salaries to
the owners. In a growth company sales grow more rapidly than
the general economy. Although the company is profitable the
owners still need to invest more funds in the business than
are being generated internally. To reduce the risk of financial
setbacks, a growth company should no longer depend on just
one or a few customers or products. Furthermore, to control
expansion, the company should have well-organized operations
and information systems. The growth phase can last from a
few months to several years depending on the potential of the
market and the ability of management to take advantage of its
opportunities.

Companies C and D represent typical growth companies. Both businesses are experiencing rapid sales growth. Company C still does not earn enough to fully finance its sales growth from internal earnings, but its basic financial condition is sound, its customer base is reasonably diversified, and day-to-day operations are well-controlled. Company D is a growing service business that is able to increase sales rapidly and still throw off more cash than it needs to support growth. It needs few assets other than accounts receivable because, as a service business, it doesn't require inventory or a lot of equipment. The only difference between company D and a mature business is that company D's sales are still increasing rapidly and management has not developed the standardized operating procedures that should characterize a stable, mature enterprise.

MATURITY

The primary favorable characteristic of a mature business is its ability to act as a cash cow to its owners. Since sales growth is moderate, the mature company should need relatively small amounts of additional investment to maintain efficient, competitive operations. If you are the owner of a mature business, you should be able to take relatively large amounts of cash out of the company to recover your prior investments. You can then use this cash for personal consumption or to fund new investments. This is the ultimate phase of financial accomplishment for the successful company owner.

A mature company must have well-established operating procedures as well as complete information for management control and planning. Even a mature business that is not growing rapidly needs substantial effort and thought to remain an efficient cash producer.

Companies E and F are both mature. Although they are in completely different industries, they have the same basic cash flow characteristics and present roughly the same type of opportunity and challenge to their owners. Neither company's sales and earnings are increasing rapidly, but both are able to produce more earnings than they need to retain in the business and both have stable financial positions with strong balance sheets. The owners of these companies can reap the financial rewards of their prior investments and efforts.

The main challenge for company E is to establish professional operating procedures that reduce its dependence on the skills and efforts of its owner. The key factor here, as in many cases, is to upgrade the abilities and motivation of middle managers. Although it is in a position to generate lots of excess cash, company E is in a cyclical industry. It must therefore constantly manage fixed costs, asset utilization, and accounts receivable to avoid serious cash flow reversals if a recession hits its industry or local economy.

Cyclical business conditions are not a serious threat in company F's industry. The owner invested a lot of time and money to develop middle managers who can operate the company without her day-to-day involvement. As in most mature businesses, Company F's profit margins have a tendency to erode. To avoid this, management must constantly monitor financial results and actively motivate employees to achieve profitability targets. Since sales are only increasing at about the rate of inflation, any substantial increase in fixed costs will also directly reduce the excess cash flow that distinguishes this business as mature.

DECLINE

Unfortunately, not all businesses that reach a stage of profitable maturity can stay that way forever—or even for very long in some cases! There are many examples of falls from the lofty heights of business success among both large public companies and small private ones. Decline in the fortunes of businesses, as in the fortunes of nations and people, is rarely the result of a single catastrophic event. Decline is usually caused by a series of seemingly small events that cumulatively cause a large decrease in performance.

The primary symptom of business decline is reduced sales volume. This is often accompanied by loss of part of the customer base. If management information is inadequate, this can happen slowly without the owner's knowledge. Sometimes it is an outside party who points it out. Either separately or in conjunction with sales declines, many companies also experience profit margin declines over time. If this results from industry conditions beyond the owner's control, a major change in strategic business direction might be needed. Often, however, profit margins, like sales, decline slowly without the owner's knowledge until one day the cash cow stops producing.

In the last two examples of Table 2–3, companies G and H are businesses that have been around many years and once made large amounts of money for their owners. Although its industry is growing, lack of management attention in company G has allowed sales to decline and the customer base to shrink. Gross profit margins remain at former levels, but net earnings have fallen below break-even because sales declined while fixed costs remained constant. The problems increased because management lacked the complete information needed to decide on remedies to improve the business. If management doesn't rapidly identify the causes of its sales decline and find a way to turn it around, company G will need to make special efforts simply to remain alive, much less to return to a profitable maturity phase.

The problem at company H is not nearly so severe. Although sales have stagnated due to competitive pressure, they have not actually declined. Profit margins went down because management made too many business decisions that yielded inadequate returns on investment and failed to cut losses by eliminating money-losing operations. This company later shed its money-losing operations and after increased investment in promotion and staff development achieved new levels of sales and profitability.

CYCLES OUTSIDE THE BUSINESS

The cycles that occur within a company are generally subject to the owner's eventual control. But cycles that occur outside individual businesses are too large to be controlled by any single company. Forward-thinking managers can, however, anticipate them. In this way they can benefit from changing conditions or at least mitigate their impact. External cycles include

1. General economic conditions.
2. Demographic, social, and political trends.
3. Individual product and technology life cycles.

Every business, no matter how large or small, is part of an overall economy that goes through cycles of expansion followed by stagnation or contraction. Despite periodic recessions, the United States has experienced a long-run trend toward expansion and greater production. At the same time, subsections of an economy, such as particular geographic areas or industries, may go through cycles that are in or out of phase with the overall economy.

In some businesses, especially small ones, sales growth rates may double or triple revenue every year. Business owners sometimes expect such growth to occur in the foreseeable future. However, no business can grow indefinitely at a rate faster than the overall industry or economy in which it operates or it would quickly grow to absorb its entire industry and economy. To date, no business in the United States has done that! Economists generally estimate that the potential growth rate for the U.S. economy, after adjusting for inflation, is only a little more than 3 percent annually. The fact that many industries and individual businesses are growing at much faster rates indicates that a lot of other businesses and industries are growing more slowly than the economy or are in a state of decline.

Some business owners fail to accept that their businesses operate as components of a larger whole. It then comes as a rude surprise when the growth of demand for their products or services eventually declines. Although the U.S. economy has generally grown throughout its history, the last 150 years have seen more than 25 periods of economic decline. During such declines even the most successful businesses will be challenged to prevent earnings and cash flow from decreasing.

Businesses that produce products or services that people use daily, such as food or utilities, are said to be relatively "recession-proof." But even though the demand for such products may not go down as much as the overall economy, the profit they generate may decline as competitors attempt to maintain growth or market share by dropping their prices. Aggressive companies that grow by taking market share away from competitors sometimes see their sales growth grind to a halt when they have driven weaker competitors from the market and are left to face only the strong.

Different kinds of economic cycles have a variety of cash flow implications. In a growth company whose sales have suddenly stopped increasing, operating costs generally go down more slowly than sales. At first management rationalizes the decline in sales as a temporary situation and therefore hesitates to cut costs. Table 2–4 shows what happened to a growth company when changes in the industry suddenly stopped its growth. In years 1 through 5 sales and gross profit increased steadily. Since operating expenses on average grew less rapidly than sales, overall operating profit increased from a loss in year 1 to a healthy profit by year 4. The first sign of weakness occurred in year 5 when operating expenses grew more rapidly than sales. This set the stage for a major problem in year 6 when sales and gross profit declined faster than management could cut fixed expenses. The result was an operating loss. When management contained the increases in operating expenses, sales started slowly upward again and profitability returned. If the rate of increase in gross profit in the following years is the same as the increase in year 7, this business will return to its previous profitability. But then it will be a mature business rather than a growth business.

If you anticipate a recession that will reduce demand for your product, you must maintain tight control over inventory or accounts receivable levels. Even when information indicates that future sales are likely to decline, many business owners habitually maintain inventory levels that exceed actual needs. This results in low liquidity and high interest costs. Eventually profit margins will suffer if prices must be cut to reduce inventory. When sales are likely to decline, you should therefore retain more than the usual amount of cash in your business rather than using your earnings to replace everything as it is sold. If your company is not actually losing money during a recession, you can generate large amounts of cash by reducing

TABLE 2–4
Changing Fortunes of a Growth Company

	Year 1	Year 2	Year 3	Year 4	Year 5	Year 6	Year 7
Sales	$2,000,000	$3,660,000	$6,015,000	$8,650,000	$9,100,000	$8,450,000	$8,700,000
Gross profit	600,000	1,160,000	1,530,000	2,200,000	2,490,000	2,080,000	2,260,000
Operating expenses	630,000	1,150,000	1,400,000	1,890,000	2,200,000	2,110,000	2,175,000
Operating income	$ (30,000)	$ 10,000	$ 130,000	$ 310,000	$ 290,000	$ (30,000)	$ 85,000

inventories and receivables. You can use this cash to pay for ongoing expenses during the downturn and to pay for new inventory or staff as you prepare for an eventual recovery.

Some businesses grow and prosper as a result of demographic, social, and political trends. If you are operating a retail or personal-service business in an area where the population is rapidly increasing, you may find it easy to realize rapid growth in sales and earnings. Likewise, if you sell products or services to highway contractors when government is spending more on roads and bridges, your business may experience a take-off. Although it's great to benefit from these kinds of trends, your business may not stay profitable once the demographic or political cycle changes or more competitors start to take advantage of the situation.

Finally, most products and technologies sooner or later yield to new ones. Be realistic about the probable duration of your product's life span in the market. Develop a pipeline of new offerings to replace or supplement older products to maintain adequate sales volume over time.

CHAPTER 3

HAS YOUR BUSINESS REALLY EVER MADE ANY MONEY?

Most business owners consider their businesses profitable whenever the expenses they choose to report in their accounting systems are less than the revenue they collect during the same time period. But this measure of profit is not enough for business owners who really want to make appropriate financial returns from their entrepreneurial efforts because it ignores some important aspects of business financial success.

Earlier we looked at the concept of opportunity cost: the amount of money that you could have earned if you had invested in something other than your own business. Before you, as a business owner, can say with certainty, "Yes, my business really is profitable," you'll need to examine opportunity cost further and measure several other aspects of business performance as well.

WHAT ARE PROFITS?

In a closely held business, as in any other financial investment, profit means more than simply taking in more money than goes out during a given period. And it also usually means more than increasing net worth Although both of these situations are favorable, they don't always indicate profitability A business should be considered

> *Unprofitable* whenever it is earning a lower annual return on investment than other investments of comparable risk

Normally profitable whenever it is earning the same annual return on investment as other investments of comparable risk.

Highly profitable whenever it is earning a greater return on investment than other investments of comparable risk.

Suppose that in 1987 a business owner has $500,000 invested in a private company. In most cases this figure would be derived from the stockholder equity portion of the company's balance sheet based on the value of the firm's assets minus any liabilities. This measure of investment may, as previously discussed, underestimate the owner's very real investment of *sweat equity* or the appreciation of property owned by the business. But for general purposes it is a useful point to begin calculating the owner's return on investment. Assume that this business is essentially mature and does not need to retain much of its earnings for reinvestment.

Now suppose that at the end of the year this business's financial statements show a net income, commonly called "profit," of $35,000 after compensating the business owner for work performed during the year or use of any of her assets, such as real property. Using conventional logic the owner sees that her company earned $35,000 over and above her compensation and declares the business to be profitable.

But if we calculate the owner's return on equity, we find that the annual rate of return on the invested $500,000 is only 7 percent (net income of $35,000 divided by stockholder equity of $500,000). By looking at a standard source of financial information like *The Wall Street Journal*, we find that anyone who invested in a long-term U.S. Treasury bond during 1987 would have been able to earn almost 9 percent. Not only would the rate of return from the government bond be greater than it was from the private business, but the investment would be less risky and easier to sell.

Compared with alternative investment opportunities, a 7 percent annual return on investment in a risky, closely held business asset cannot be considered adequate for 1987. Therefore, even though this business had a positive net income and, presumably, a positive cash flow, it has to be considered unprofitable because it did not earn an adequate return on investment for its owner.

BENCHMARKS OF PROFITABILITY

What annual rate of return should you look for on an investment in your own business?

Determining an appropriate annual rate of return is something of an art as well as a matter of individual judgment and philosophy. Financial analysts, academicians, and other knowledgeable professionals often differ widely on the exact rate of return that they consider adequate for a particular business at a particular point in time. Several theories and techniques have been developed to calculate the appropriate rate of return for a business in a given situation. Although many of these methods have merit, they are usually difficult for most business owners to apply. Also, return on investment measures tend to go in and out of vogue depending on the current conventional wisdom either within a particular industry or the general financial and investment community.

This doesn't mean that you'll have to hire high-priced advisers to assess the true profitability of your business. A number of readily available financial indicators can serve as benchmarks from which to measure the performance of your own unique private business investment relative to the performance of other investments.

START WITH RETURN ON EQUITY

One place to start is with the annual return on stockholder equity (ROE) earned by publicly traded companies. These data are readily available in various statistical sources and annual surveys in business magazines. Some of these figures are more reliable than others, depending on the industry segment a company is in. You'll need to carefully analyze the reported ROE for industries that are largely service oriented because their relatively few assets tend to make their ROEs quite high. Likewise, the ROE figures reported for natural resource companies or companies with valuable property carried at low historical costs tend to be deceptive.

To establish a general benchmark for typical ROE on a broad sample of companies, let's look at the averages calculated for U.S. manufacturing companies by the U.S. Department of Commerce (Table 3–1). This information indicates that for the 10 years ending in 1987, U.S. manufacturing companies earned, on average, a 12.4 percent annual return on their stockholder equity (capital plus retained earnings). Although the ROE varies considerably over the 10-year period, the annual ROE for these companies as a group was never less than 9.2 percent. Furthermore, the historic averages for ROEs in manufacturing companies as far back as 1947 are virtually identical to those of the last 10 years. Keep in mind that these are after-tax returns. The average annual pretax ROE for these companies probably exceeds 17 percent.

Naturally these average ROE figures include companies with various degrees of financial success. The more successful companies are obviously earning more than a 12.3 percent return on stockholder equity. Aggressive industry leaders such

TABLE 3–1
Return on Equity for All
Manufacturing Corporations

Year	ROE
1978	15.0%
1979	16.4
1980	13.9
1981	13.6
1982	9.2
1983	10.6
1984	12.5
1985	10.1
1986	9.5
1987	13.1
1978–87	12.4

Source: U.S. Department of Commerce, Bureau of the Census.

as IBM and General Electric strive for, and have achieved, after-tax ROEs of more than 20 percent. These big companies are financially secure, they have a small probability of financial failure, and their publicly traded stock is easily marketable.

If relatively low-risk public companies are earning more, sometimes much more, than a 12 percent annual return on their stockholders' equity, shouldn't the owners of riskier, less liquid private companies expect to earn even more? Calculate the ROE for your own business. If it isn't higher than the amounts earned by the less risky public companies in similar industries, are you really making a profit?

TYPICAL INVESTORS' RETURNS

People who invest in the public stock and bond markets expect to receive a return on their investment that reflects the degree of risk and other characteristics associated with each potential investment. A well-accepted financial principle is that, as the amount of risk associated with an investment increases, the rate of return expected by a rational investor will likewise increase. And many studies indicate that in the long run there is a positive correlation between the ROE earned by a company and the value that investors place on its stock.

Most financial analysts consider U.S. Treasury securities to be the least risky financial investment. The U.S. government has an excellent credit history, vast resources for paying its debts, and active worldwide markets for quickly trading its issues. Therefore, the rate of return available for U.S. government securities tends to create a floor above which all investments must rise to provide an adequate rate of return for investors.

Because investment in a private company is usually made for an indefinite, generally long period of time, looking at investors' annual rate of return on long-term U.S. Treasury bonds is a logical starting point. Table 3–2 shows the approximate annual yield available to investors from long-term U.S. Treasury bonds during the years 1978 through 1987. The average annual rate of return for this period was 10.7 percent. That annual rate of return is about 3 percent more than the 6.6 percent average annual rate of inflation during the same period.

TABLE 3–2
Long-Term U.S. Securities
Approximate Average
Annual Yield

Year	Yield
1978	8.9%
1979	10.2
1980	12.5
1981	13.7
1982	10.6
1983	12.0
1984	11.6
1985	9.8
1986	8.4
1987	8.9
1978–87	10.7

In other words, since 1978 investors buying long-term U.S. Treasury bonds expected to receive an average rate of return about 3 percent more than the general rate of inflation. Studies over long time periods have shown that this is the rate of return in excess of inflation that an investor who assumes no risk expects to receive.

Stock market investments are always considered riskier than investment in U.S. Treasury securities. Empirical studies of the long-term average spread between the return on U.S. Treasury securities and the return on investment in the stock of major corporations such as those represented by the Dow Jones Averages and the Standard & Poor's 500 Index indicate that over long time periods investments in the common stock of major public companies can be expected to return an average premium of three to seven percentage points more than the annual return on U.S. Treasury securities.[*]

The Standard & Poor's 500 is a group of 500 public companies from all segments of the U.S. economy. The S&P 500 Index measures the change in the value of these companies' stocks.

---

*See, for example, Ibbotson and Sinquefield (1976), Stocks, Bonds, Bills, and Inflation: Year-by-Year Historical Returns (1926–1974); *Journal of Business, 49*, and subsequent updates.

The annual change in that index provides us with a measure of the rate of return based on stock values that investors receive from year to year. Table 3–3 shows the yearly change since 1978 in the S&P Index's average annual value. For the entire 10 years the average annual change has been a 10.6 percent increase in value. In addition to the general rise in value over time, these stocks also provide dividend payments that have yielded a 10-year average annual return of 4.7 percent. Therefore, the total annual return available to stock market investors—value appreciation plus dividends—as measured by the S&P 500 from 1978 through 1987 has been about 15.3 percent. The year-to-year returns on these stocks have been much more variable (i.e., risky!) than the rate of return on U.S. Treasury securities. But the average annual return has been almost 5 percent higher than risk-free investments, which is consistent with the financial theory.

SO WHAT?

All these historical data and theories have an important message for you as the owner of a closely held company if you want

TABLE 3–3
Standard & Poor's 500 Stock Index

Year	Annual Change In Value[*]	Dividend Yield	Total Annual Return[†]
1978	1.1%	5.3%	6.3%
1979	12.3	5.5	17.8
1980	25.8	5.3	31.0
1981	−9.7	5.2	−4.5
1982	14.8	5.8	20.6
1983	17.3	4.4	21.7
1984	1.4	4.6	6.0
1985	26.3	4.3	30.6
1986	14.6	3.5	18.1
1987	2.0	3.1	5.1
1978–87 Mean	10.6	4.7	15.3

[*]Based on year-end value.
[†]Change in value plus dividend yield.

to know whether you are making an adequate return on *your* investment. Small, private companies, even well-established ones, are always a risky investment for several reasons:

1. Their earnings can vary dramatically from year to year.
2. They typically have fewer financial and managerial resources to draw on than larger companies.
3. They often experience greater competitive pressure and greater risk of business failure than major publicly traded companies.
4. They represent an intrinsically illiquid investment. Owners who want to sell their stock may not find a ready market, and, if they do, the amount and timing of payment are often open to question.

Therefore, if you want to consider your company truly profitable, you'll need to earn a higher average rate of return than the rates investors earn in the public stock market. Otherwise you are probably losing money.

THINK ABOUT HOW YOUR BUSINESS MAKES MONEY

Like stock market investors, private business owners can receive financial returns from their investments in two basic forms: *capital appreciation* (or capital gains) and *ordinary income*. Most business owners or investors know these terms because of their former federal income tax connotations. Before 1987 capital gains were taxed at a lower rate than ordinary income. This concept is now generally obsolete for income tax purposes, but the distinction between these two types of earnings can still help you plan how to cash in the chips from private business investment.

The value of your business or its assets may increase from one year to the next. When that happens, you are earning money through capital appreciation. All other things equal, businesses increase in value if they are profitable going concerns with increasing sales and earnings. And sometimes part of a business's assets will be real estate or other property that also tends to increase in value. After a number of years the owners of a successful company may have earned a sizable amount of income through increases in the value of their business or its assets.

Many business owners naively assume that, as long as they keep the doors open, their businesses are increasing in value. This is not always true. During the 1970s this mistaken assumption often appeared to be true simply because sales and earnings increased due to high rates of inflation. The lower inflation of the 1980s made the lack of real growth in many private companies obvious. In many cases the increase in business values subsequently slowed. Even if your business is vigorous and expanding, your assets can stop growing after a while and, depending on the phase of your business's life cycle, its value can actually go into decline. Business values are like stock values: what goes up *can* come down.

Business owners can also earn returns on their investments in the form of dividends, either formal or informal. For good reasons most small private companies do not pay formal dividends per se. But a successful private company should have a *dividend-paying capacity*. Such a capacity can be measured as either cash or other assets accumulated by the business that are not needed for day-to-day operations or reinvestment to keep the basic business running. When such excess cash or assets are available, they can be distributed to the owners as a kind of informal dividend. This is not the same as the owner's salary. It includes any income from the business that is *more* than the market value of either the owners' managerial efforts or the use of their other assets by the business.

If you want to realize the maximum return from your business investment, you need to consider whether you want to make money primarily by capital appreciation or by "dividend" income. Unless your business is able to grow rapidly without the support of reinvested earnings, you may not be able to earn money by both means at the same time. To develop a plan that will give the best return on your investment, you'll need to know where your company lies on the continuum between a pure *holding* company and a pure *operating* company. A pure holding company might be one whose only asset is a piece of raw land that is increasing in value. A pure operating company might be a sole practitioner attorney who earns income only when he personally delivers a service. Your best strategy will depend on the type of business you own.

If your business is primarily a holding company, you probably buy assets such as real estate or natural resources and keep them while, with good fortune, they appreciate in value over a number of years. In such a situation a strong capital appreciation strategy will be appropriate. I have seen businesses such as plant nurseries, day care centers, or building material supply outlets that have operated for years with little or no profit reflected on their income statements. But in fact the meager earnings from the operations were being used to make payments on well-located real estate that was appreciating rapidly due to urban expansion. A common shortcoming with such strategies occurs when the owners fail to keep accurate track of the rate at which their assets are appreciating. They may not realize that the annual rate of increase in their property value has slowed to less than the rate of return they could be earning elsewhere.

Companies that are primarily operating businesses generally increase in value as a result of their sales and earnings rather than their physical assets. If your business is primarily an operating company, you will probably want to plow back most of your earnings into expanding your business as long as the market opportunity for your product or service is profitably increasing. All other things being equal, the value of your company should continue to increase more or less proportionately to its earnings and cash flow. But even if you have taken relatively little income out of your business, you need to let potential buyers know that this option is available. Again, it is important to monitor the rate of return on your investment. Don't continue plowing money back into your business when growth in earnings levels off. Your return on investment will decline if you are retaining earnings at a faster rate than sales and income are increasing.

A FEW CASE STUDIES

Tables 3–4, 3–5, and 3–6 show the income, cash flow, and other derived profitability information for three different private com-

TABLE 3–4
Easy Flow Industries

	1982	1983	1984	1985	1986	1987	1982–1987 Average
A. Basic Facts							
Sales	$7,240,000	$9,000,000	$10,430,000	$10,290,000	$9,700,000	$9,500,000	
Expenses	6,901,746	8,573,937	9,836,713	9,745,493	9,307,647	9,067,325	
Net income	338,254	426,063	593,287	544,507	392,353	432,675	$477,777
Cash	127,774	164,883	189,168	187,413	178,993	174,372	
Noncash assets	1,936,954	2,586,722	2,798,359	2,954,932	2,896,979	3,235,191	
Total assets	$2,064,728	$2,751,605	$ 2,987,527	$ 3,142,345	$3,075,972	$3,409,563	
Liabilities	293,279	665,043	743,363	614,309	485,828	675,123	
Stockholders' equity	$1,771,449	$2,086,562	$ 2,244,164	$ 2,528,036	$2,590,144	$2,734,440	
Net income equity	19.1%	22.1%	27.4%	22.8%	15.3%	16.3%	20.8%
B. Cash Flow Summary							
Net income		$ 426,063	$ 593,287	$ 544,507	$ 392,353	$ 432,675	
− Change in noncash assets		649,768	211,637	156,573	(57,953)	338,212	
+ Change in liabilities		371,764	78,320	(129,054)	(128,481)	189,295	
= Cash flow		148,059	459,970	258,880	321,825	283,758	$294,498
+ Beginning cash		127,774	164,883	189,168	187,413	178,993	
− Free cash*		110,950	435,686	260,634	330,245	288,380	285,179
= Ending cash†		164,883	189,168	187,413	178,993	174,372	

TABLE 3–4—Continued

	1982	1983	1984	1985	1986	1987	1982–1987 Average
C. Market Value							
Esimated market value	$3,551,667	$4,473,662	$6,229,514	$5,717,324	$4,119,707	$4,543,088	
Change in estimated market value		26.0%	39.2%	-8.2%	-27.9%	10.3%	5.0%
Free cash/estimated market value		2.4	7.0	4.5	8.0	6.3	5.7
Total return to owners		28.4%	46.2%	-3.7%	-19.9%	16.6%	10.7%
D. S&P Index							
Change in value		17.3%	1.4%	26.3%	14.6%	2.0%	12.3%
Dividend yield		4.4	4.6	4.3	3.5	3.1	4.0
Total return		21.7%	6.0%	30.6%	18.1%	5.1%	16.3%
Long-term U.S. Treasury yield		12.0%	11.6%	9.8%	8.4%	8.9%	10.1%

*Cash not needed for business operations that can be distributed to owners.
†Cash retained in the business to support operations.

TABLE 3-5
High Rise Distributors

	1982	1983	1984	1985	1986	1987	1982–1987 Average
				A. Basic Facts			
Sales	$1,640,000	$4,260,000	$5,470,000	$9,450,000	$8,350,000	$8,530,000	
Expenses	1,540,414	4,096,533	5,322,166	9,199,157	8,121,113	8,296,179	
Net income	99,586	163,467	147,834	250,843	228,887	233,821	$204,970
Cash	118,278	41,702	102,349	176,907	156,175	159,542	
Noncash assets	250,178	533,663	591,865	1,267,049	1,114,722	1,127,789	
Total assets	$ 368,456	$ 575,365	$ 694,214	$1,443,956	$1,270,897	$1,287,331	
Liabilities	241,260	284,702	418,281	1,024,792	690,048	478,944	
Stockholders' equity	$ 127,196	$ 290,663	$ 275,933	$ 419,164	$ 580,849	$ 808,387	
Net income equity	78.3%	78.2%	52.2%	72.2%	45.8%	33.7%	56.4%
				B. Cash Flow Summary			
Net income		$ 163,467	$ 147,834	$ 250,843	$ 228,887	$ 233,821	
− Change in noncash assets		283,485	58,202	675,184	(152,327)	13,067	
+ Change in liabilities		43,442	133,579	606,511	(334,744)	(211,104)	
= Cash flow		(76,576)	223,211	182,170	46,470	9,650	$ 76,985
+ Beginning cash		118,278	41,702	102,349	176,907	156,175	
− Free cash*		0	162,564	107,612	67,202	6,283	68,732
= Ending cash†		41,702	102,349	176,907	156,175	159,542	

TABLE 3-5—Continued

	1982	1983	1984	1985	1986	1987	1982–1987 Average
C. Market Value							
Estimated market value	$717,019	$1,176,963	$1,064,405	$1,806,071	$1,647,989	$1,683,515	
Change in estimated market value		64.1%	−9.6%	69.7%	−8.8%	2.2%	18.6%
Free cash/estimated market value		0.0	15.3	6.0	4.1	0.4	5.1
Total return to owners		64.1%	5.7%	75.6%	−4.7%	2.5%	23.8%
D. S&P Index							
Change in value		17.3%	1.4%	26.3%	14.6%	2.0%	12.3%
Dividend yield		4.4	4.6	4.3	3.5	3.1	4.0
Total return		21.7%	6.0%	30.6%	18.1%	5.1%	16.3%
Long-term U.S. Treasury yield		12.0%	11.6%	9.8%	8.4%	8.9%	10.1%

*Cash not needed for business operations that can be distributed to owners.
†Cash retained in the business to support operations.

TABLE 3-6 Tropical Notions

	1982	1983	1984	1985	1986	1987	1982–1987 Average
A. Basic Facts							
Sales	$3,660,000	$6,010,000	$8,660,000	$9,100,000	$8,440,000	$8,450,000	
Expenses	3,613,000	5,869,000	8,422,000	8,836,000	8,455,000	8,350,878	
Net income	47,000	141,000	238,000	264,000	(15,000)	99,122	$145,424
Cash	196,000	489,083	161,962	169,923	72,923	160,594	
Noncash assets	447,000	1,443,000	2,499,000	2,606,000	1,950,000	2,263,000	
Total assets	$ 643,000	$1,932,063	$2,660,982	$2,775,923	$2,022,923	$2,423,594	
Liabilities	686,000	1,932,000	2,480,000	2,357,000	1,619,000	1,923,000	
Stockholders' equity	$ (43,000)	$ 83	$ 180,962	$ 418,923	$ 403,923	$ 500,594	
Net income equity	−109.3%	NM	262.9%	88.0%	−3.6%	21.9%	73.8%
B. Cash Flow Summary							
Net income		$ 141,000	$ 238,000	$ 264,000	$ (15,000)	$ 99,122	
− Change in noncash assets		996,000	1,056,000	107,000	(656,000)	313,000	
+ Change in liabilities		1,246,000	548,000	(123,000)	(738,000)	304,000	
= Cash flow		391,000	(270,000)	34,000	(97,000)	90,122	
+ Beginning cash		196,000	489,083	161,962	169,923	72,923	
− Free cash*		97,917	57,122	26,038	0	2,452	$ 29,624
= Ending cash†		489,083	161,962	169,923	72,923	160,594	36,706

TABLE 3-6—Continued

	1982	1983	1984	1985	1986	1987	1982–1987 Average
			C. Market Value				
Estimated market value	$ 329,000	$ 987,000	$1,666,000	$1,848,000	$ 945,000	$1,090,683	
Change in estimated market value		200.0%	68.8%	10.9%	−48.9%	15.4%	27.1%
Free cash/estimated market value		9.9	3.4	1.4	0.0	0.2	3.0
Total return to owners		209.9%	72.2%	12.3%	−48.9%	15.6%	30.1%
			D. S&P Index				
Change in value		17.3%	1.4%	26.3%	14.6%	2.0%	12.3%
Dividend yield		4.4	4.6	4.3	3.5	3.1	4.0
Total return		21.7%	6.0%	30.6%	18.1%	5.1%	16.3%
Long-term U.S. Treasury yield		12.0%	11.6%	9.8%	8.4%	8.9%	10.1%

*Cash not needed for business operations that can be distributed to owners.
†Cash retained in the business to support operations.

57

panies during a six-year time period from 1982 through 1987. The three companies have experienced various rates of sales and earnings growth and have differing financial structures. During the six-year period each of the companies experienced both growth and decline in sales and earnings. These examples will establish a measure of each company's profitability over a representative part of its business cycle. In no case, however, can the profitability story be considered complete. Depending on business opportunities and management decisions, each company could go on to be more (or less) profitable in the future than it has been in the past.

In section A of each table are the basic facts about each company as they are derived from typical financial statements. The average annual and five-year ROEs based on the book value of stockholder equity for each business are also calculated.

Overall cash flow is calculated in section B of each table. These measurements take into account not just earnings but also the use of cash associated with changes in each company's assets and liabilities. All the sample businesses have lower levels of cash flow than earnings during the time period covered because to various degrees they are buying new assets to support growth or they are reducing liabilities. In each case the amount of *free cash* available each year has been calculated. Free cash is the amount of cash available each year that is not considered necessary to retain in the business to support operations and meet anticipated obligations. Free cash is money that the owners should be able to withdraw from the business in one form or another and is considered a measure of dividend-paying capacity.

In section C each company's annual market value is estimated based on an analysis of the individual businesses as well as conditions in each particular industry and the overall investment market. All these businesses have a strong service component, so their market values tend to be high relative to assets and stockholder equity. The business owners' estimated annual total return on investment is also summarized in section C. The percentage by which the value of the business changes from one year to another represents the rate of capital gain or loss to the owner. The free cash generated as a percentage of the estimated market value of the business is the equivalent of a dividend yield. The sum of these two percentages represents the owner's total rate of return from the business during the year.

The total return from the stock market, as represented by the Standard & Poor's 500, and the average annual yield on long-term U.S. Treasury securities for the years in question are summarized in section D. This summary provides a benchmark to measure the subject company's relative performance and profitability to its owners. Because private companies are intrinsically more risky than public ones, their owners should expect to receive a greater average rate of return than they could earn from alternative investments.

THE CASH COW

Easy Flow Industries in Table 3–4 is almost a classic cash cow. It has been in business for several decades. But during recent years sales and income have peaked and then declined. As a result, the company has experienced no net growth in sales or earnings. Despite the lack of real growth, however, this company has consistently generated substantial free cash flow for its owners. For the five years ending in 1987 average free cash flow was equal to almost 60 percent of average net income. And the annual return on stockholder equity averaged more than 20 percent for the years 1982 through 1987, although the trend for ROE has been generally downward. Many people would look at the substantial annual free cash flow generated by Easy Flow, averaging about $285,000 annually during the last five years, and declare the business profitable. But other factors must be considered before drawing such a conclusion.

Section C, which shows the owners' overall return on investment, indicates that Easy Flow has not been highly profitable compared with alternative investments. Because its sales and earnings didn't increase much after 1983, the company's net value has grown at an average of only 5 percent annually since the end of 1982. The free cash flow available to stockholders has averaged an effective yield equal to 5.7 percent of the company's market value. Free cash has held up well despite declines in earnings. The total return to the owners over five years based on an increase in the value of the business plus the effective cash yield is estimated to average about 10.7 percent annually.

During this same period long-term U.S. Treasury investments yielded an annual average of about 10.1 percent. And in the stock market the S&P 500 returned an average of more than 16 percent annually to investors. Although this was an unusually favorable period in the stock market, the return to owners of this private company, being only about 0.6 percent greater than the return on government securities, cannot really be considered profitable. Long-run investments in the stock market would be expected to yield much more than Treasuries.

Besides not earning much more than they would receive from risk-free Treasury bonds, the owners of Easy Flow have no liquidity in their investment and face the responsibilities and difficulties of operating their own business. Later we'll look at some methods that this company might use to increase its return on investment. But for now I would judge Easy Flow to be unprofitable when compared to its opportunity cost

A HIGH ROE SITUATION

Table 3–5 tells us about High Rise Distributors, a fast-growing business that used borrowed money to finance a large part of its growth. The company began to pay down those borrowings when its business growth leveled off. High Rise has consistently had a positive net income, and with a relatively small amount of stockholder equity it has earned a very high average ROE. Even as earnings leveled off after 1985 annual ROE has been well over 30 percent. And the average earnings for the last five years, about $205,000, divided by the ending equity of about $808,000, imply an ability to continue earning an average ROE of at least 25 percent in the future.

Free cash flow in this situation has not been consistent enough for High Rise to be considered a cash cow, but it has the potential to become one. Although it was highly leveraged during the last five years, High Rise needed considerable funds to support asset growth and pay off prior liabilities. On average only about 34 percent of net income has been available as free cash flow. This is much less than the percentage available from a cash cow like Easy Flow, but High Rise still has a fairly large, although fluctuating, annual dividend-paying capacity for its owners.

High Rise's average annual increase in market value for the five-year period has been 18.6 percent, and its yield of free cash flow to market value has averaged 5.1 percent. This total estimated annual rate of return to the owners, 23.7 percent, is about 2.4 times more than the return on U.S. Treasury securities for the last five years and about 1.5 times greater than the S&P 500 total return. Given that High Rise has reduced its overall financial risk as measured by the ratio of liabilities to equity and assuming that earnings and free cash flow will remain at least at present levels, my overall judgment is that this company has been quite profitable.

With astute management, this company may continue earning high total returns for its owners. High Rise may be able to continue its profitable growth trend with high ROE and reasonable free cash flow. Or, if growth opportunities are limited, the company should be able to substantially increase its payout of free cash flow as a percentage of net income and market value by keeping the ratio of liabilities to equity relatively constant.

A HIGH FLYER WITH
A QUESTIONABLE OUTLOOK

Tropical Notions, illustrated in Table 3–6, grew rapidly with even greater leverage than High Rise used. Consequently it has even more variable net income and cash flow. Its average ROE is extremely high due to a relatively small amount of stockholder equity. But Tropical Notions' risk is also high because its debt is almost four times the value of its total assets.

Financial performance has been erratic. In its most profitable years Tropical Notions has shown an ability to produce a fair amount of free cash flow as well as rapid appreciation in its estimated market value. But conditions in its principal market became more difficult. As the company's annual sales declined, its net income and free cash flow declined much more rapidly due to the high degree of debt and other fixed costs.

The overall profitability question for this company is difficult to answer with certainty. Strictly speaking, Tropical Notions' five-year average total return to its owners as calculated in section C of Table 3–6 is 30.1 percent. That appears high compared to the market benchmarks. But clearly almost all this return was earned during the earlier years, and the company's level of risk is still quite high because of the large debt load. If Tropical Notions can return to its earlier sales and earnings growth pattern, then its market value should grow again. But, if it doesn't grow substantially, the company has little chance to prudently generate much free cash flow in the near future because of the need to service debts.

Although this company has been, on average, highly profitable to its owners since 1982, it has still shown an overall negative return since the end of 1985. Its uncertain earnings outlook indicates that Tropical Notions may have insufficient future profitability to compensate for its inherent risk and lack of liquidity. The best option for maximizing future returns to the owner in this situation may be to sell out now if possible and invest the proceeds in other opportunities

DON'T ALWAYS TAKE YOUR FINANCIAL STATEMENTS AT FACE VALUE

In a well-run business, financial statements—primarily the income statement and balance sheet—should be complete, accurate, and up-to-date in terms of conventional accounting standards. Such statements provide a solid baseline for developing information useful for making management decisions as well as meeting obligations to financial institutions and tax authorities. But when it comes to measuring a business's profitability, it is frequently necessary to make adjustments to conventional accounting statements in order to get a more com plete picture of what is happening.

A typical situation in which standard accounting needs to be adjusted to obtain a sharper measure of profitability is shown in Table 3–7. Column A shows a business balance sheet and income statement as reported by standard accounting methods. The company, Typco, Inc., is reported to have $1,300,000 in assets and $600,000 in stockholder equity. Annual pretax income is $205,000, which indicates that Typco is apparently highly profitable with a 34.2 percent pretax return on stockholder equity. But additional analysis indicates that this profitability calculation, although correct by standard accounting conventions, greatly overstates both the degree and source of profitability.

Several adjustments must be made to Typco's accounting so that it better represents what is actually happening in the business. First of all, in most cases standard accounting methods show the *book* value of fixed assets—their original cost minus any accumulated depreciation, a measure that is frequently based on relatively arbitrary tax-reporting methods. In this example Typco has land and buildings with a book value of only $600,000 while in fact the property was purchased a number of years ago and is now worth much more. A real estate appraisal indicates Typco's property is actually worth $1,000,000, which is $400,000 more than its book value. This adjustment is made in column B. Given the actual value of its real estate, Typco actually owns $1,700,000 in assets, and the stockholder equity in those assets is $1,000,000.

Typco's income statement also needs some adjustments to measure true profitability. The owner's compensation of $120,000 is the amount of salary and benefits that the owner is able to take out of the company. But the market value of the owner's labor, that is, the amount that a competent nonowner-manager would be paid to do the same job, is estimated to be only about $80,000. Also, because the company owns its business property, it doesn't show any rent on its income statement. But, if Typco weren't using the building, it could be renting it out to someone else. The rent Typco is *not* collecting is therefore an opportunity cost. Based on the property appraisal, the market value of rent for Typco's use of the building is $100,000 per year, and this amount is shown as an adjustment in column B

TABLE 3–7
Typco, Inc.

	A 198X as Reported	B Adjustments	C Adjusted 198X Performance
	Balance Sheet		
Current assets	$ 200,000		$ 200,000
Equipment	500,000		500,000
Land and buildings	600,000	$400,000*	1,000,000
Total assets	$1,300,000		$1,700,000
Liabilities	700,000		700,000
Stockholder equity	600,000		1,000,000
Liabilities and equity	$1,300,000		$1,700,000
	Income Statement		
Sales	$2,500,000		$2,500,000
COS	1,625,000		1,625,000
Gross profit	$ 875,000		$ 875,000
Operating expenses			
Owner compensation	120,000	$ (40,000)[†]	80,000
Rent	0	100,000[‡]	100,000
Other	550,000		550,000
Total operating expenses	670,000		730,000
Pretax income	$ 205,000		$ 145,000
Annual change in property value		50,000[§]	50,000
Pretax income + Change in property value			$ 195,000
Pretax:			
Return on sales	8.2%		5.8%
Return on assets	15.8%		8.5%
Return on equity	34.2%		14.5%

Return on equity, including
    net income + Change
    in property value
			19.5%

[*]Based on current appraisal.
[†]Adjust to reasonable market value.
[‡]Estimated from property value.
[§]Estimated from current market conditions.

After making these two expense adjustments, we can see in column C that the company's adjusted pretax income from its operations is realistically only $145,000 rather than $205,000. And the earnings from these operations amount to a rate of return of only 14.5 percent on its real stockholder equity of $1,000,000.

Typco has an additional nonoperating source of income not recorded on the standard accounting statements. During the year, Typco's property appreciated by an estimated $50,000. This increase in value partly offsets the rent expense, meaning that Typco's owners really had total pretax earnings for the year of $195,000.

It might seem at first that the final pretax income of $195,000 is only about 5 percent less than the initial book income of $205,000. But this $195,000 was earned from a real stockholder equity investment of $1,000,000. Therefore, the adjusted pretax return on equity is only 19.5 percent. Although this is a fairly favorable amount, it is only a little more than half as profitable as the rate of return reported in the financial statements. And, if the company's real estate stops appreciating as much as it did this year, Typco's return on equity from operations, 14.5 percent, may not be enough to be considered profitable when compared with investment alternatives.

In calculating the true profitability of your business, you will probably have to consider adjusting three financial statement items:

1. Asset values.
2. Owner or family member compensation.
3. Rental value of property and equipment owned by the business owner.

In the real world I see examples of accounting systems that overstate income in some manner about as often as I see those that understate income. Many businesses show a positive net income but are not really profitable because the owners or their families are not able to take out as much salary as they would pay someone else to perform the same work. Businesses like these may actually be thought of as losing money. In other cases, despite a positive net income and an apparently sufficient annual rate of return, a business may have no free cash flow for years on end because debts must be paid off or new assets have to be purchased to remain competitive.

PROFESSIONAL SERVICE BUSINESS PROFITABILITY

Measuring profitability in professional service businesses requires a different approach from that used for other companies. Most professional service businesses such as law firms, accounting firms, medical practices, consultancies, architectural firms, and technical writing services, have few assets and little equity from which to measure a rate of return. In many cases a professional service business has limited salability or, even if the business is salable, its value may peak and level off many years before the practitioner is ready to sell.

The best measure of profitability for a professional service business, then, is free cash flow measured against the market salary and benefits that the practitioner/owner would be likely to earn from someone else under comparable conditions. In this kind of business free cash flow is represented by the *draws* the owner can take out of the business after providing for working capital requirements, replacing equipment, and servicing debts.

Figure 3–1 shows the rolling annual income (the sum of earnings for the prior 12 months) for a professional service business plotted over five years. The solid, upward-sloping line is the amount of income and benefits, including expected raises, that the owner felt she would be able to make if she practiced her profession as an employee for someone else. It begins at about $30,000 per year and ramps up to around $45,000 four years later. The actual 12-month rolling income line, which is the amount of money the owner was able to draw out of her business, is somewhat erratic but has a generally upward trend. During the first year she earned only about $11,000 over 12 months, which was much less than her $30,000 opportunity cost. Therefore this business was clearly unprofitable. By the third year her income began to roughly track with the amount she could make working for someone else Only during the

FIGURE 3–1
Service Business Rolling 12-Month Income

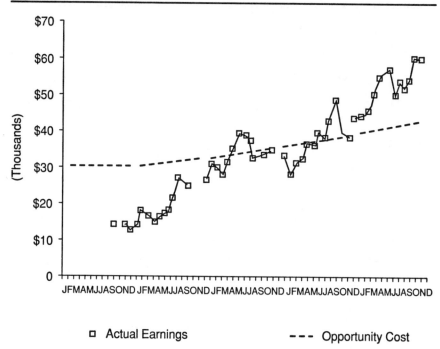

middle of the fifth year when her income began to average more
than $50,000 annually was this business starting to be truly
profitable for its owner.

This perception of profitability is only valid if the owner's
actual earnings include a provision for such things as additional
self-employment taxes, retirement contributions, and health
insurance, that would typically be paid for by an employer.
Assuming the service business's income figures include all the
benefits that an employer would provide, by the middle of year
5 the owner is making, on average, about 35 percent more than
her opportunity cost. Depending on the degree of risk associated
with being self-employed as compared to working for someone
else (which in this day of frequent mergers and "reductions in
force" may not be all that much!) this business has apparently
turned the corner in terms of profitability for its owner.

FIGURE 3–2
Service Business Cumulative Income

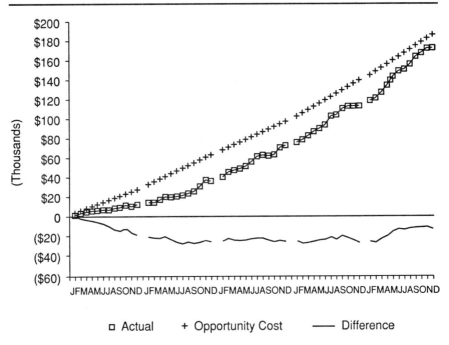

☐ Actual   + Opportunity Cost   —— Difference

Another perspective on the same service business is shown in Figure 3–2. These lines measure the cumulative total of actual income and opportunity cost since the beginning of the business. When the total opportunity cost is subtracted from the business's total actual income at any point in time, the resulting difference represents the cumulative profit or loss to the owner. Even though we have seen that the owner's annual income has exceeded her opportunity cost by about 35 percent since the middle of the fifth year, there is still a cumulative loss in this business. In other words, so far the sum of all money earned through self-employment is still not equal to the sum of all the money the owner would have earned by working for someone else. Only when the cumulative actual income starts to exceed the cumulative opportunity cost, which will probably occur during the sixth year if these trends continue, will it be possible to argue that this business has been profitable in the sense that it has repaid the owner's opportunity cost. By tracking these trends in the future, the owner will be able to assess whether her service business is still making money or whether she should consider, at least for financial reasons, practicing her profession as an employee of someone else.

CHAPTER 4

QUESTIONS OF VALUE

Finance professors in university business schools teach their students that the primary business objective of professional managers is to maximize the value of their companies to their respective stockholders. There is evidence that this mission is taken seriously among the public companies represented on the leading stock exchanges and the investors and analysts who follow those companies. When its stock value falls, a public company often becomes prey to new owners and managers who can, or at least think they can, produce greater value and return on investment for stockholders.

When polled, private business owners as a group do not list the desire to maximize financial returns as their primary objective for going into business. Entrepreneurs usually cite such reasons as an intrinsic interest in their business's product or service, a desire for independence, or a drive to create something that didn't exist before. It is perfectly reasonable for private business owners to have objectives in addition to maximizing the value of their companies. But the question of value creation cannot be ignored.

Nonbusiness owners who want to retire comfortably have to build up the value of their savings or pension fund investments throughout their working years. Few people are able to save enough money to retire after just a couple of years of investing. Personal financial planners advise their clients to calculate how much income they will need to live on when they retire, and use that to estimate how large a "nest egg" they need to accumulate over the years.

As a private business owner, your company is probably your most valuable asset, and you very likely depend on it in one way or another to provide a comfortable retirement income. To provide such a nest egg, your business must produce enough free cash flow to accomplish one or more of the following:

1. Provide a pension fund.
2. Pay dividends after you are no longer active in management.
3. Net enough after-tax cash in a sale to provide capital for retirement funds.

If you hope to fund your retirement by the eventual sale of your business, you'll need to calculate ahead of time how much the business will need to be worth at the anticipated retirement date to meet your projected retirement needs. If for no other reason than this, you must regularly monitor the value and salability of your business. If it is not appreciating sufficiently, then you will have to change direction or take steps to improve the situation. If it doesn't have the potential to provide the income level you need for retirement, then you may want to sell early and reinvest the proceeds in another asset that will meet your needs or seek other employment. Increasing the value of a business takes many years. It is just as impractical to try to fund your retirement by increasing the value of your business in only two or three years as it is to rely on quick returns from any other investment.

HOW PROFESSIONALS LOOK AT BUSINESS VALUE

Stock analysts, professional investors, and business appraisers base their opinions of a business's value primarily on the amount and timing of its earnings or cash flow.

> How much money will I receive, when will I receive it, and in what form will I receive it if I make an investment in this business? And what will be my annual rate of return on that investment?

From this perspective, a business derives its value from its ability to provide a stream of cash flow that exceeds the need to plow money back into the company for reinvestment. This is what we have referred to as free cash flow.

If you are calculating the value of your business based on its earnings ability, you may not need to consider the value of physical assets (measured either as the original amount paid, replacement cost, or market value) such as inventory, equipment, real property, and so forth. The important thing is not how much you paid for your business's assets but how much the person who controls those assets can earn.

This is why professionals typically use price/earnings (P/E) ratios to determine value. In other words, they look at the price, or value, of a business as a function of its annual earnings. There may be more than one definition of earnings for this purpose. The earnings figure used might be net income, as it is in the published figures for the stock market, or another measure such as pretax income or some definition of cash flow. For example, a given business at a particular point in time might be described as being worth 8 times pretax earnings or 12 times net income.

Some P/E ratios are based on the figures available for publicly traded companies similar to the company being valued. Others are based on actual sales transactions within a particular industry as reported by investment bankers, business brokers, or published research materials. In many instances, however, no information on appropriate P/E ratios will be available for a particular private business. If your business falls into this category, you will have to develop your own P/E ratios.

As we discussed in Chapter 3, if you are an owner of or investor in a private company, you should expect to earn more than someone who invests in less risky, publicly traded stocks. To calculate the appropriate P/E ratio for your business, first determine the expected annual rate of return on investment. If your business is mature and you don't expect its earnings to grow any faster than inflation, then the inverse of the expected rate of return may be the appropriate P/E ratio. Look at Table 4–1 in the example under the column that has no rate of growth. The expected rate of return based on the assumptions used

TABLE 4–1
Converting Expected Rate of Return to Price/Earnings Ratios

	Growth Rate Categories			
	None	*Moderate*	*High*	*Very High*
Long-term Treasury yield[*]	9.0%	9.0%	9.0%	9.0%
Public stock market premium[†]	5.0%	5.0%	5.0%	5.0%
Closely held business risk premium[‡]	5.0%	5.0%	5.0%	5.0%
Expected rate of return	19.0%	19.0%	19.0%	19.0%
− Real growth rate[§]	0.0%	5.0%	10.0%	15.0%
= Net capitalization rate	19.0%	14.0%	9.0%	4.0%
Price/earnings ratio[‖]	5.3	7.1	11.1	25.0

[*]Based on current market rate.

[†]Average actual long-term results based on academic studies.

[‡]Judgment; this would vary depending on the degree of risk associated with a given business.

[§]The expected long-term average annual increase in earnings after taking inflation into account. This tends to decline as a business matures.

[‖]The P/E ratio is calculated by dividing 1 by the net capitalization.

is 19 percent. The inverse of this percentage is 5.3 (i.e., 1/.19). Buyers who want to earn a 19 percent annual return on their business investments in a company with no growth prospects would be willing to pay 5.3 times that business's annual net income. If they paid more than that, they would earn a lower return on investment than they desire.

On the stock market and in business acquisitions, we often see P/E ratios of 10, 12, 15, or more times earnings. Just as the inverse of the expected rate of return is the P/E ratio, the inverse of the P/E ratio must be equal to the expected rate of return. Does this imply that a person buying a business for 12 times annual income is satisfied with only an 8.3 percent (1/12) annual rate of return? Not really.

The inverse of the P/E ratio is the rate of return after considering anticipated long-term annual earnings growth. If a business earns $100,000 today but is expected to grow because, for instance, the demand for its product is increasing faster than the general rate of inflation, then the anticipated annual rate of growth should be subtracted from the required return to calculate the correct P/E ratio. All other things being equal, a company with earnings growth warrants a higher P/E ratio than a similar company whose earnings are not growing. In the second column of Table 4–1 we see that an investor who wants a 19 percent rate of return and anticipates annual earnings growth of 5 percent more than inflation in the business he or she wants to buy, then the anticipated net capitalization rate is 14 percent. This converts into a P/E ratio of 7.1 times current earnings (1/.14). As a company's expected growth rate increases, with all else equal, its P/E ratio should likewise increase.

Buyers should be cautious in extrapolating very high current rates of growth indefinitely into the future. When companies or markets are new, they can easily grow at high annual percentage rates because the base from which the firm is growing is so small. But as companies increase in size, they usually have fewer profitable growth opportunities and the annual rate of growth inevitably declines. Business owners, especially when they are sellers, tend to be highly optimistic about their companies' chances for indefinite double-digit annual rates of sales and earnings growth. But realistically the average business's long-term annual growth prospects, after adjusting for the effects of inflation, are less than 5 percent per year. That is because for the United States as a whole the feasible, sustainable after-inflation growth rate as calculated by numerous economic studies is only somewhat more than 3 percent annually. As we mentioned earlier, any business that grew indefinitely at a much faster rate than its surrounding business environment would eventually absorb the entire economy of its city, region, or country.

WHY SIMILAR BUSINESSES
MAY HAVE DIFFERENT VALUES

Look at the facts regarding two wholesale distribution businesses in Table 4–2. Progressive Distributors can be expected to earn an annual net income of $100,000 after allowing for management compensation, replacement of worn-out equipment, and the like. Under present market conditions, an investor

TABLE 4-2
Progressive Distributors versus Upstate Distributors

	Progressive	Upstate
Assets	$1,000,000	$1,300,000
Liabilities	500,000	500,000
Net worth	$ 500,000	$ 800,000
Annual net income	$ 100,000	$ 100,000
Return on equity	20.0%	12.5%
Expected rate of return	16.0%	16.0%
Market value based on earnings*	$ 625,000	$ 625,000
Actual return on equity/ expected rate of return	1.3	0.8

*Annual net income divided by expected rate of return.

should expect to earn a 16 percent annual rate of return in this particular business. Therefore a buyer should be willing to pay $625,000 for Progressive. This is because $100,000 per year in earnings represents a 16 percent annual return on a $625,000 investment. This is true even though the net book value of Progressive's physical assets is only $500,000. The owner should expect to receive $625,000 because, if Progressive were sold for only $500,000, the buyer would be earning a 20 percent annual return when only a 16 percent rate of return is expected.

Upstate Distributors in Table 4-2 also earns an annual net income of $100,000. Upstate used to have greater annual sales and earnings than it does today and therefore has built up a larger asset base than Progressive. But Upstate's sales and earnings have declined due to competitive pressure, and now it earns about the same amount of money as Progressive. Based on its annual earnings and a 16 percent expected rate of return, Upstate is also estimated to be worth $625,000 as a going concern. Upstate may in fact be worth more "dead than alive." That is, unless the owner can find a way to increase net income to at least $128,000, which represents a 16 percent annual return on the company's $800,000 net worth, he could make more money by liquidating the company's assets than by selling it as a going concern.

The difference, if any, between the net value of a company's physical assets and a higher market value as a going concern is commonly referred to as *goodwill*. However, I prefer the term *going concern value* or *intangible value*. That's because "goodwill" implies that there is an intrinsic value to a business's friendly, continuing relationship with customers regardless of whether that business has ever made a real profit or is ever likely to make one. Some business owners think they deserve to sell their companies for more than their asset values simply because they have survived a number of years without declaring bankruptcy. But a business really has intangible value only when it earns owners a rate of return greater than the amount expected based on the value of the owners' investment in physical assets alone.

Table 4–3 compares Progressive Distributors and Mid-Cities Distributors. Both companies are in the same business, are the same size in terms of annual sales, and have substantially identical assets and debt structure. But Progressive is able to earn $100,000 per year from its assets while Mid-City earns only $80,000. Although both companies have the same net worth, the going concern value in the market for Progressive should be $125,000 greater than Mid-City's. This $125,000 in additional value may be attributed to Progressive's intangible assets or, if you like, its goodwill. To be certain that these

TABLE 4–3
Progressive Distributors versus Mid-City Distributors

	Progressive	*Mid-City*
Assets	$1,000,000	$1,000,000
Liabilities	500,000	500,000
Net worth	$ 500,000	$ 500,000
Annual net income	$ 100,000	$ 80,000
Return on equity	20.0%	16.0%
Expected rate of return	16.0%	16.0%
Market value based on earnings[*]	$ 625,000	$ 500,000
Actual return on equity/ expected rate of return	1.3	1.0

[*]Annual net income divided by expected rate of return.

intangible assets are worth their implied value, the buyer or business appraiser needs to specifically identify why Progressive is able to earn more than Mid-City. It is also important to ascertain that this advantage can be transferred from the company's present owner to a prospective buyer.

Progressive could be making more money than Mid-City simply because it is located in a lower-rent facility. Or perhaps Progressive has better trained employees, sells a product line with higher profit margins, or is more efficient due to computerized order processing and stricter credit requirements. All these factors can probably be transferred to a new owner and therefore support a market value that, based on Progressive's earnings, is substantially more than its net asset value.

Mid-City's owner may say in all sincerity that her business has goodwill value because it has had many years of continuous friendly relationships with its customers. But there is no evidence that those years of congenial business relationships have accomplished anything that allows Mid-City to earn more than the basic rate of return that should be expected from its investment in physical assets. Therefore it is not possible from these facts to argue that Mid-City has any intangible assets or a going concern value that is greater than its net asset value.

ACTUAL P/E RATIOS PAID IN THE MARKET

Finding accurate information about the P/E ratios that are actually paid for private companies is obviously difficult. Such facts are generally not made public. One industry source is W.T. Grimm & Co. in Chicago, which maintains a database of facts regarding both public and (anonymous) private transactions in the United States merger and acquisition market. Their data sample for private transactions, shown in Figure 4–1, is based on figures from hundreds of transactions involving relatively large private companies (over $5 million in value). Although the information won't necessarily apply to small private companies, it still provides a benchmark for actual transactions. And the average P/E ratios reported very likely represent the value that sellers of larger private companies can expect to receive.

FIGURE 4–1
Price/Earnings Ratios as Reported by W.T. Grimm & Co.

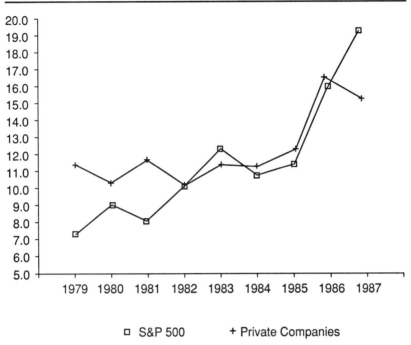

□ S&P 500   + Private Companies

The figures in Table 4–4 indicate that the average price of all the private company sale transactions from 1979 through 1987 was 6.8 times pretax earnings. Except for the two most recent years, which were very high bull market years in the investment community, the P/Es were fairly consistent from year to year. The trend of the P/E ratios for the private companies generally follows the trend of P/E ratios for public stock acquisitions and the stock market as a whole. Because P/E ratios for the stock market were generally lower in 1988 than the prior year, the values of private companies that are sold will probably be lower as well.

Also notice that the P/E ratios paid for private companies were lower in each year than the P/E ratios paid for public companies. This might be because most private companies never develop the depth of management and organization typical of their public counterparts. But it may reflect the tendency

TABLE 4–4
Estimated Pretax P/E Ratio[*]

Year	Private Companies	Public Companies
1979	6.1	6.3
1980	5.6	6.1
1981	6.2	6.9
1982	5.5	6.5
1983	6.2	7.8
1984	6.2	7.7
1985	6.6	7.9
1986	8.9	9.9
1987	10.0	13.1
Mean	6.8	8.0

[*]Derived from price/earnings ratios reported by W.T. Grimm & Co., Chicago. Calculated on the assumption that the average company was in the highest marginal corporate tax rate during the year.

of larger companies to sell for higher earnings multiples than smaller companies, as W.T. Grimm has reported. This is presumably because larger companies typically have lower business risk due to their greater financial resources and market clout.

Although the average estimated pretax price of these private companies from 1979 through 1987 was 6.8 times earnings, there was considerable variation within the group. During that nine-year period at least 15 percent of the companies sold for less than five times pretax earnings while 36 percent of the companies sold for more than nine times pretax earnings. The trend through 1987 was for fewer businesses to sell for the lowest P/E ratios, but this may not apply directly to the market for smaller businesses since generally only the larger or more successful private companies tend to show up on this survey. Nevertheless, these valuation ratios provide some targets to shoot for in the attempt to create maximum value for your business.

As a practical matter business brokers indicate that the smallest classes of private companies, the so called Mom-and-

Pop businesses, typically sell for lower earnings multiples than those reported for larger transactions. One reason is the risk that small businesses typically run because of their heavy dependence on one or two employees and their high sensitivity to seemingly minor changes in their local market, which may cause large shifts in sales and earnings. Such small companies are typically sold to buyers of limited means, and, right or wrong, their value may be limited by the ability of prospective buyers to arrange financing.

KEYS TO A BUSINESS'S INTRINSIC VALUE

Most people would agree that in modern Western societies all of us need money to survive. But at a fundamental level rational people know that money has little or no intrinsic value. What they really want are the things they think money can buy such as food, shelter, amusement, security, and maybe some form of happiness. People's standards of living are measured less by the quantity of money they have than by the amount of comfort, health, or security their money can provide.

Just as people need money to obtain the other things they really want, businesses need assets such as cash, inventory, and equipment to generate sales and earnings for their owners. But those assets may have little or no intrinsic value outside of their ability to generate sales and earnings. The key to the value of most businesses is not the current net value of their assets but the ability of those assets to generate cash that can be distributed to the owners. When rational investors determine how much they are willing to pay for a private business, the principal characteristics they should consider are not the resale value and condition of such assets as inventory and equipment but the income those assets will generate.

In extreme situations successful businesses have virtually no tangible assets. A few years ago, in an article about the Calvin Klein fashion company, *Fortune* magazine wrote that, according to the company's chief operating officer, the business earns many millions of dollars each year for its owners but has virtually no physical assets. Calvin Klein has no manufacturing equipment because all its clothing production is either sub-contracted or handled by licensees. It has very little inventory because most of its products are made to order and delivered directly to customers. Because fashion merchandise may have a very short salable life, at the end of each month the company clears any remaining inventory out of its rented warehouses at reduced prices. The owners of Calvin Klein realize that a balance sheet full of inventory and equipment provides little value to them when they can make large amounts of money without investing in such assets.

The key to creating business value is not necessarily accumulating business assets. The key to building value is creating an organization that can convert its assets into revenue, earnings, and cash flow that eventually exceeds the cash originally invested in business assets. In one way or another, business owners must measure this expected stream of earnings to determine what their businesses are worth.

Valuing a business on its earnings involves much more than counting up the cash, inventory, accounts receivable, equipment, and buildings and then subtracting the liabilities to determine net worth. Most importantly, it involves tracking the business's earning and cash-generating power. Although imperfect, several means of measuring earning power are available to business owners. But these measurements aren't ends in themselves. The information they provide should be used, if possible, to help maximize a company's value.

Historical Earnings

How much money has the business earned for its owners in the past? According to the historical earnings assumption, a track record of prior earnings indicates how much the business will earn in the future. It is important to consider not only how much the company is earning but also whether there is an upward or downward trend or a great degree of variability from year to year. An upward earnings trend that is likely to continue will be more valuable than an earnings trend that is flat or declining. And a highly variable stream of income should be considered riskier and therefore less valuable than a more predictable one. The best demonstration of high value in a business is a regular and increasing stream of cash flow that exceeds the expected rate of return on physical assets.

Expected or Projected Earnings

If a business is new or otherwise likely to grow substantially beyond its present size, historical earnings may understate the earnings that owners can expect in the future. In this case, future earnings can be estimated by making a sales projection and multiplying it by the typical net profit margin for the particular company or the company's industry in general. But there is a drawback to this approach. As potential sellers, business owners tend to be overly optimistic about their expected earnings, so buyers are naturally skeptical of measurements not based on historic performance.

Sales Trends

Sales trends are the basic source of all business earnings. Someone has to be willing to pay for a company's products or services if the business is ever going to make more money than it started with. An upward sales trend therefore provides some evidence that future earnings will be greater than present or past earnings.

Many private business owners indicate that they eventually hope to sell their businesses, but few appear to manage their companies over the years with that goal in mind. In many instances business owners assume they can make some quick-fix improvements or accounting changes shortly before putting their companies on the market and thereby realize top dollar for their life's work It is amazingly common for business owners who have never achieved any great financial success to tell prospective buyers that their businesses are worth far more than their net asset value because based on the work of the current owner the buyer can "easily" make 2 times (or 10 times!) more money than the current owner ever has. On the other hand, some owners of businesses with meager net asset values assume that their companies have little other intrinsic value. The following examples of two small manufacturing concerns show how mistaken both of these perspectives can be.

Table 4–5 summarizes the financial facts for Bluesky Manufacturing, a small manufacturing job shop making components on contract to larger companies. The owner of this company wanted to sell it for much more than its $310,000 net worth and justified the asking price by pointing out that the business had been operating many years and was well-known to potential customers. He wanted to receive at least $400,000 in order to retire. But Bluesky's meager profits give no evidence of net sales growth in the last three years. Also, even though the company has virtually no debt, it is a highly risky enterprise because almost all its sales go to one customer. Net income in 1988 was $45,000, but the average annual earnings for the past three years, $33,000, have to be considered typical of future earnings potential due to lack of demonstrated sales growth and the competitive nature of the industry. Based on its average performance, Bluesky earns only a 10.6 percent rate of return on its reported net worth of $310,000. A prospective buyer of Bluesky should want to earn at least between a 15 and 20 percent annual rate of return and therefore would rationally pay no more than 5 to 6.7 times earnings since the company shows no growth trend. Even if the prospective buyer made the most optimistic assumptions by applying a P/E ratio of 6.7 to the most recent year's earnings of $45,000, the value of the business would be only $301,500. Based on the average annual earnings of $33,000, Bluesky is worth even less, perhaps only $225,000. The company's owner in this case is not likely to get nearly as much money as he would like because his business earns too little to justify even its basic investment in physical assets.

Specialty Manufacturing in Table 4–6 is in virtually the opposite situation. It has lower asset and net worth values than Bluesky, but because it is highly efficient at making a specialized product, it earns an extremely high rate of return on its equity. Assuming Specialty has the same overall risk and growth prospects as Bluesky, the same P/E ratios of 5 to 6.7 could reasonably be used to value the business. Applying these P/E ratios to the average annual net income of approximately $72,000 indicates a value between about $360,000 and $480,000. This amount is two to three times the company's reported net

TABLE 4–5
Bluesky Manufacturing, Inc.

	1986	1987	1988	Annual Average
Sales	$1,460,000	$1,250,000	$1,330,000	$1,346,667
Net income	34,000	20,000	45,000	33,000
Total assets	280,000	282,000	317,000	
Total liabilities	13,000	19,000	7,000	
Net worth	$ 267,000	$ 263,000	$ 310,000	
Return on sales	2.3%	1.6%	3.4%	2.5%
Return on equity	12.7%	7.6%	14.5%	10.6%

TABLE 4–6
Specialty Manufacturing, Inc.

	1986	1987	1988	Annual Average
Sales	$453,000	$487,000	$504,000	$481,333
Net income	65,000	76,459	73,584	71,681
Total assets	186,000	198,000	207,000	
Total liabilities	34,000	37,000	43,000	
Net worth	$152,000	$161,000	$164,000	
Return on sales	14.3%	15.7%	14.6%	14.9%
Return on equity	42.8%	47.5%	44.9%	43.7%

worth, but it may be quite reasonable because of the extremely high—43.7 percent—average annual return on equity that Specialty has earned for the past three years. Ironically, the owner of this business considered selling it for less than $200,000, despite the probability of substantial sales growth, because of the company's relatively low tangible net worth.

OPERATING COMPANIES VERSUS ASSET COMPANIES

As we mentioned in Chapter 3, most businesses fall somewhere along a continuum from a pure operating company to a pure asset-based or holding company. The closer to the pure operating end of the spectrum a business lies, the more emphasis should be given to revenue and earnings trends as the primary indication of value. In such a business, assets are valuable only insofar as they create more revenue and earnings. The Calvin Klein example mentioned previously is a case in point.

The closer a business is to the pure asset-holding end of the spectrum, however, the more important is the resale value of its assets. Such physical assets as land, buildings, or equipment may have more value to a potential buyer for another purpose than the business operations conducted by the current owner. For example, a buyer might decide to convert a farm to an industrial park because the value of the land as a location for other commercial activity may be far greater than the capitalized value of the earnings from agriculture on that land.

For most businesses the source of value falls somewhere closer to the middle of the operations-assets spectrum. In many cases owners can maximize their total business value by selling the operating portion of the business separately from some of its assets. To use a typical example, a company might be operating a "lower-level" business such as manufacturing or wholesaling from a piece of real estate that could be rented to a "higher-level" business such as a retail or consumer service. The business operations, which are valued on their earnings, might be just as profitable at a lower-rent location, while the land is valued on its highest and best use as retail property. The owner of this company could sell the operations to a buyer willing to relocate and the land to a buyer willing to make more profitable use of it. The value of the sum of these parts may therefore be greater than the whole.

VERY SMALL BUSINESSES AND PROFESSIONAL PRACTICES

The basic valuation principles outlined in the previous section are commonly used by investment analysts. Although they represent reasonable approaches, however, they aren't often used in actual transactions of the smallest businesses and professional practices. Many very small companies make little or no money after compensating their owners for the hours they work. Therefore such businesses have no earnings to capitalize. From the professional analyst's return-on-investment point of view, then, their assets may not be worth the money initially paid for them. Nonetheless, these companies frequently do sell. And, even though their value is frequently limited to the estimated market value of their physical assets, buyers can at times be convinced to pay more. The real trick to obtaining value from these smallest of businesses may lie more in finding a motivated and qualified buyer than in achieving any particular financial performance objective.

People are often willing to purchase small businesses based on their ability to produce what is sometimes referred to as *owners' discretionary cash flow*. This measurement of cash flow is typically defined as the amount of money a business generates after paying all its expenses *except* a salary to the owner, depreciation, and interest on debt service. This approach assumes that small business owners have a degree of discretion about what to pay themselves, whether to pay off long-term debts or refinance them, and whether to replace equipment at the rate it is depreciated for tax purposes. Whether this measurement is really "discretionary," that is, fully under the owner's control, is debatable. But it does indicate the amount of money that can in theory be taken out of the business. Keep in mind that paying for such a business, either as the founder or as a subsequent buyer, may be no more than just buying a job.

Professional service businesses such as CPA practices, insurance brokerages, or medical and dental practices are frequently valued in relation to their annual billings at the time of sale. Despite the stated price, the buyer usually spreads the payments over a number of years, basing them on the fees of clients who are actually retained in the new practice. Although such a method again appears to fly in the face of professional return-on-investment approaches, it is not so unreasonable if the payments are viewed as royalties or commissions to compensate the seller for the business being referred to the new practitioner. For example, although the business may have been valued on the basis of one times its annual revenue, if the payments are spread over, say, five years, they really amount to a 20 percent royalty for all the business transferred during the period of the agreement. From the buyer's viewpoint this may be a relatively inexpensive method to build up profitable additional business volume.

BEWARE OF INDUSTRY "RULES OF THUMB"

Many industries have traditional formulas that are often used to determine the business value. These formulas are frequently based on some multiple of revenue or the physical volume of product sold rather than earnings or cash flow–generating capacity. It can be highly risky to rely on industry formulas as the only indication of business value.

A few years ago I reviewed a situation in which a beverage distributor had been valued on what was supposedly a widely used industry formula. According to this formula, distributors should be worth an amount equal to the number of cases of beverages they distribute each year times a certain number of dollars per case. In this case, the formula grossly overvalued the business because its primary market was a rural area that required a lot more driving (and therefore higher vehicle-operating expenses and driver salaries) to distribute a given amount of beverages than would be the case in a metropolitan area. Because operating costs per case were higher, the company's earnings on a given business volume were less than those of a comparable distributor in a more urbanized area. Obviously such a formula might also undervalue a distributor in a market that was highly economical to serve.

Industry formulas would be reliable if every business in a given industry had the same business volume, the same profit margins, identical overhead, and consistent rates of annual sales growth. But that is simply not the case even in relatively standardized businesses such as national franchise chains. Each company has individual differences that affect its earnings and return on investment. As long as that is the case, blindly relying on a "standard" formula rather than carefully analyzing the facts in each situation is not likely to result in a correct business value except by chance.

THE ULTIMATE REALITY OF VALUE: IS THERE A QUALIFIED BUYER?

Calculating the value of your business in a professional manner can be a useful exercise both for planning your value-maximizing strategy and for ensuring fair compensation when it comes time to sell. But when you're actually ready to cash in your chips, it takes two parties to complete the transaction. A successful company may have a high value based on its return on investment to the owner but can't find a buyer interested in taking on the business at that price. Or someone may be willing to pay the price but only on *easy terms*, which in effect substantially reduce the amount the seller is receiving. And in some cases there may be very few, possibly only one or two, qualified buyers. So always be willing at least to consider valid proposals to purchase your business. If nothing else, you'll get additional market information about what your company is worth.

CHAPTER 5

SETTING MEANINGFUL BUSINESS OBJECTIVES

Once upon a time a business owner subsisted on meager wages and spent thousands of hours developing his company and its product. Although he made occasional sales to customers, the big year was always going to be next year when his product was finally perfected and really ready to promote and sell. Larger companies who wanted to sell his product now occasionally made offers to purchase the business, but the owner felt those offers were never high enough. He justified his current losses as the price he had to pay to have a better market position and company in the future. But in the meantime technology and customer trends were changing, and by the time the business owner's product was perfected few people wanted it. The years of losses were never regained, and nobody wanted to buy the business anymore.

A frequent critical theme in both the popular and academic business press is that the management of public companies and investment analysts put too much emphasis on short-term financial performance to the detriment of longer-term benefits. No doubt some of this criticism is warranted. But some managers, and particularly the owners of private companies, tend to defend themselves from charges of poor business performance by claiming that their short-term earnings are poor because they are really positioning their businesses for better long-term growth and earnings. It is difficult to know for certain whether business owners who forgo current earnings and cash flow in an attempt to create a better financial future are really making a good investment or are just fooling themselves about future prospects.

Think of the people who decide they need to lose some excess weight and become more physically fit in order to be healthier when they are older. If these people fail to meet correct eating and exercise standards on a daily basis, they are unlikely to achieve their eventual goals. Consistent failure to meet short-term performance targets means it will eventually be impossible to achieve the desired long-term results. As the old Chinese proverb says, "If you don't change direction, you will end up where you are going."

It is important to build for the future and get ready to meet strategic challenges and changing market conditions. But long-term business performance, say over several years or the entire life of a company, is no more than the sum of all the periods of short-term performance. And each short-term period that falls short of profitability will delay and possibly reduce the likelihood of eventual long-term financial success. If your business is experiencing short-term negative cash flows or earnings levels that are too low to justify your business investment, you'll need to take an objective look at the situation and set specific short-term goals. That way you can be more certain that you will recover your investments and find enough chips on the table to collect when you are ready.

ESTABLISHING PERFORMANCE TARGETS

To increase the chances that your business will succeed in the long term, you need to establish earnings targets for each short-term period. As an owner and senior manager, you may want to measure results on a quarterly or annual basis, but you must also translate your goals into both terms and time periods that are meaningful to all employees on a day-to-day basis. For example, telling some managers or most employees that they need to improve profit margins or increase return on assets is not particularly useful. These may be important ingredients in reaching your eventual business goals, but they are not easy to convert into meaningful daily or weekly activity. The best way to do this is to develop some practical equations that describe the way your business makes money. This lets you identify *levers* that can be measured and pulled to improve your company's performance. Once you've identified these important levers, you can establish objectives for achieving profitability targets and monitor your progress toward them.

The basic profitability equation for measuring, understanding, and improving return on equity (ROE) in your business is

$$\overset{A}{\underset{\text{Sales}}{\text{Net income}}} \times \overset{B}{\underset{\text{Assets}}{\text{Sales}}} \times \overset{C}{\underset{\text{Equity}}{\text{Assets}}} = \overset{D}{\text{ROE}}$$

The first part of the equation, net income/sales, represents a business's profit margin as a percentage of sales, sometimes called net profit margin. The greater this ratio is, the more profitable the business will be. Therefore maintaining or improving this ratio should be an important short-term and long-term objective. The management of Variety Manufacturing, Table 5–1, has not only increased its annual sales substantially but also concentrated on improving profit margins. The result is that over five years the company raised its profit margin from less than 2 percent to more than 7 percent. It did this by such means as investing in more productive machinery, improving credit checks to reduce bad debt, and reducing interest expenses. By concentrating on meeting profit margin objectives, Variety was able to quadruple its return on stockholder equity.

This contrasts strongly with the performance of HiGrowth Stores in Table 5–2. Although HiGrowth has experienced steady sales growth, its managers have not rigorously maintained control of profit margins. HiGrowth's industry is relatively predictable and mature, and therefore the company should be able to operate on small but consistent margins. By not achieving regular 1.5 percent profit margins, which are about average for its industry, HiGrowth has made about $300,000 *less* in total net income over a five-year period than it should have made.

The sales/assets ratio, part B of the return-on-equity equation, is an activity or productivity indicator. It shows how efficiently a business uses its assets to generate a given volume of sales. The factors that affect this ratio in most companies are

TABLE 5-1
Variety Manufacturing

	1984	1985	1986	1987	1988
Sales	$8,200,000	$9,700,000	$12,260,000	$14,450,000	$15,700,000
Net income	105,000	225,000	880,000	940,000	1,150,000
Assets	3,025,000	3,130,000	4,430,000	5,020,000	5,585,000
Liabilities	1,005,000	885,000	1,305,000	955,000	370,000
Equity	2,020,000	2,245,000	3,125,000	4,065,000	5,215,000
Net income/ sales	1.3%	2.3%	7.2%	6.5%	7.3%
Sales/assets	2.7	3.1	2.8	2.9	2.8
Assets/equity	1.5	1.4	1.4	1.2	1.1
Return on equity	5.2%	10.0%	28.2%	23.1%	22.1%
Assets Required with Sales/Assets Ratio of 3.0					
Adjusted assets*	$2,733,333	$3,233,333	$4,086,667	$4,816,667	$5,233,333
Actual assets minus adjusted assets†	291,667	(103,333)	343,333	203,333	351,667

* The amount of assets that would be required if a sales/assets ratio of 3.0 were maintained regularly.
† The unneeded assets in the company if the sales/assets ratio of 3.0 were maintained. If this number is positive, it is the amount that would be available to the owners for their own use.

TABLE 5–2
HiGrowth Stores, Inc.

	1984	1985	1986	1987	1988
Sales	$6,150,000	$7,800,000	$9,250,000	$11,700,000	$12,700,000
Net income	(35,000)	115,000	150,000	70,000	110,000
Assets	560,000	715,000	960,000	1,190,000	1,250,000
Liabilities	315,000	355,000	450,000	610,000	560,000
Equity	245,000	360,000	510,000	580,000	690,000
Net income/sales	−0.6%	1.5%	1.6%	0.6%	0.9%
Sales/assets	11.0	10.9	9.6	9.8	10.2
Assets/equity	2.3	2.0	1.9	2.1	1.8
Return on equity	−14.3%	31.9%	29.4%	12.1%	15.9%

Return on Equity with a Consistent Profit Margin of 1.5%

	1984	1985	1986	1987	1988
Adjusted net income*	$ 92,250	$117,000	$138,750	$ 175,500	$ 190,500
Adjusted ROE	24.8%	32.3%	27.8%	25.6%	24.7%
"Lost" income[†]	$(127,250)	$ (2,000)	$ 11,250	$(105,500)	$ (80,500)

* The amount of net income the company would have earned if a 1.5% net profit margin had been retained each year.
[†]The income each year that was lost because profit margins were not maintained.

(1) the speed at which accounts receivable and inventory are turned over and (2) the efficiency with which the business generates sales from its investment in equipment and property. All other things being equal, if a company can increase the amount of revenue it generates from a given investment in assets, it will make more free cash available for distribution to shareholders or investment in other opportunities.

At Variety Manufacturing, the use of assets as measured by the sales/assets ratio has stayed about the same over the five years, but it seems to have room for improvement. In 1985 the company was able to maintain a sales/assets ratio of 3.1; that is, for every $1.00 invested in assets, Variety generated $3.10 in sales. Why not establish a sales/assets ratio of at least 3 as a business objective for each year? This might be accomplished through improved inventory or accounts receivable management, elimination of unneeded or obsolete equipment, or more effective cash management. The lower section of Table 5–1 shows that if Variety had been able to maintain an average sales/assets ratio of 3 each year, then by the end of 1988 the company would have had about $350,000 less tied up in its business assets. Had this happened, Variety's owners would have had an additional $350,000 in cash available for their personal use or other investments.

The third ratio, assets/equity, measures a company's relative use of debt, which is sometimes called financial leverage. The assets/equity ratio shows how many dollars of assets there are for each dollar of owners' equity. The higher this ratio is, the more a company is relying on debt to support its operations. In stable businesses that are not subject to undue fluctuations in sales and earnings, it is frequently more profitable not to pay off all the company's debt as long as the return on equity exceeds the cost of borrowing money. Therefore, once a company has achieved a reasonable degree of financial stability, it may be more beneficial for its owners to take money out of the business for their own use or other investments rather than to pay off all the company's debts.

Marginal Distribution in Table 5–3 had an extremely high debt level in 1984. That financial leverage in 1984 produced a spectacular ROE of almost 64 percent, but such a high degree of debt

TABLE 5-3
Marginal Distribution, Inc.

	1984	1985	1986	1987	1988
Sales	$8,650,000	$9,100,000	$9,000,000	$8,700,000	$8,640,000
Net income	140,000	130,000	120,000	25,000	120,000
Assets	2,720,000	2,700,000	1,950,000	2,280,000	1,930,000
Liabilities	2,500,000	2,350,000	1,480,000	1,785,000	1,315,000
Equity	220,000	350,000	470,000	495,000	615,000
Net income/sales	1.6%	1.4%	1.3%	0.3%	1.4%
Sales/assets	3.2	3.4	4.6	3.8	4.5
Assets/equity	12.4	7.7	4.1	4.6	3.1
Return on equity	63.6%	37.1%	25.5%	5.1%	19.5%

Return on Equity with Assets/Equity Ratio of 4.0

	1984	1985	1986	1987	1988
Adjusted equity*	$680,000	$675,000	$487,500	$570,000	$482,500
Adjusted ROE	20.6%	19.3%	24.6%	4.4%	24.9%
"Excess" equity†	$(460,000)	$(325,000)	$(17,500)	$(75,000)	$132,500

*The amount of equity that would be required if an assets/equity ratio of 4 were maintained each year.
†The unneeded equity in the company if the assets/equity ratio of 4 were maintained. If this is a negative number, the company needs to build up more equity. But if it is a positive number, it would be available to the owners for their own use.

was risky to maintain. Since 1984 the company has reduced its debt level by retaining a substantial portion of its annual earnings. In 1988 Marginal's earnings of $120,000 were the same as in 1986, and its profit margin and sales/assets ratio were about the same in both years. However, Marginal's ROE in 1988, 19.5 percent, is much lower than it was in 1986 when the company earned the same net income. This is because Marginal reduced its assets/equity level below 4. From a return-on-equity point of view, the company may have reduced its debt too far. As the lower part of Table 5–3 shows, if Marginal had maintained a steady assets/equity ratio of 4 during the period 1984 to 1988, which in this particular industry is considered acceptable, the company would still be earning a 25 percent annual ROE. And the owners would have been able to take an additional $132,500 out of the business for their own use. Except for a slip in 1987 when sales suddenly declined, Marginal has maintained steady profit margins that are typical for its industry. And its sales/assets ratio has improved about as far as is feasible. Therefore, the best way for Marginal to improve returns to its owners may be to establish assets/equity objectives that will maximize ROE and free up cash.

Monitoring the fundamental ratios that affect ROE and setting objectives for each of them are vital steps in achieving maximum return from business investments.

CONSIDERATIONS FOR PROFESSIONAL SERVICE BUSINESSES

The kinds of financial profitability ratios discussed in the preceding section will not be meaningful if your business is a professional service or other enterprise that uses almost pure labor rather than physical assets to generate revenue and earnings. Such service businesses should determine, set objectives for, and monitor the key variables that drive their profitability. For example, once a professional service firm that charges by the hour establishes a given fixed cost structure (rent, equipment, and basic staff salaries), the only controllable variables that drive financial success are related to revenue generation. These can be reduced to an equation such as this·

$$A \qquad\qquad B \qquad\qquad C$$

$$\text{Number of clients} \times \text{Hours per client} \times \text{Avg rate per hour}$$
$$= \text{Revenue}$$

Monitoring performance on these variables over time can help the business owner determine which lever to pull to improve profitability. Table 5–4 shows how a CPA, doing business as Creative Accounting Services, was able to increase profitability over time by tracking the key variables. To achieve her income goals, the owner's practice had to generate more than $130,000 per year in revenue. The average number of hours of service her small business clients require is about the same each year. When she started her practice and didn't have a strong reputation, she could charge fees of only $50 per hour. For the first two years, she concentrated on finding new clients. Then, during the next two years, she was able to raise her hourly rates and, after some lag, increase the number of clients again. By 1987 Creative's owner had achieved her overall revenue goal, but she felt that the number of hours of work required per month was too high. So in 1988 she increased her hourly rates once more to the highest amount typically charged by similar firms in Creative's market. Although this move resulted in the loss of some clients, Creative maintained its overall annual revenue and reduced the amount of time the owner worked per month to a more manageable level. By knowing and using the key profitability levers in her business, Creative's owner made systematic business decisions that allowed her to meet her objectives.

MONITORING THE BREAK-EVEN POINT

Every business or professional practice needs to generate a certain volume of annual revenue to break even. And because a business has to achieve certain levels of profitability to be of any real value to its owner, the calculation of break-even should include a provision for an appropriate amount of profit. Most businesses have combinations of fixed and variable costs. The fixed costs (rent, management salaries, interest on debt, etc.) have to be paid regardless of how much business is being

TABLE 5-4
Creative Accounting Services

	1984	1985	1986	1987	1988
Number of clients	17	26	28	40	32
× Average hours per client	48	45	50	46	45
× Average rate per hour	$ 50	$ 75	$ 75	75	95
= Annual revenue	$40,800	$87,880	$104,832	$137,267	$136,091
Average revenue per client	$ 2,400	$ 3,380	$ 3,744	$ 3,432	$ 4,253
Average hours per month	68	98	116	153	119

conducted, whereas the variable costs usually vary as a certain percentage of business volume. The amount of money earned after subtracting variable costs from revenue is called *gross profit*, and gross profit as a percentage of revenue is known as *gross margin*. Using these definitions, the basic formula to calculate break-even for any business is

$$\frac{\text{Fixed costs + Profit goal}}{\text{Gross profit margin}} = \text{Break-even revenue}$$

A business's break-even point will change over time as its fixed costs and/or gross margin change. Earlier we saw that although HiGrowth Stores' annual revenue had increased every year, its net income was actually falling. A break-even analysis will help explain what is happening at HiGrowth and show how management could develop a plan to improve performance.

As we calculated previously, HiGrowth needed to maintain a 1.5 percent net profit margin to produce an adequate profit and return on equity for its owners. Table 5–5 and Figure 5–1 show how much annual revenue HiGrowth needs to achieve its profitability goals over a seven-year period. In only two of the past seven years was HiGrowth's actual revenue greater than the amount it needed to make the desired profit. A closer look at the data indicates that, although the company's gross margin has increased from 9.5 percent to 13 percent, HiGrowth's fixed costs have grown more rapidly than sales. Figure 5–1 shows what is happening. As sales increased every year, HiGrowth's break-even point increased even faster. Profitability became a moving target, and HiGrowth's management would have been better off to concentrate on containing expenses rather than just increasing sales. Unfortunately, once a high fixed-cost structure has been created, it is usually difficult, or at least painful, to reduce.

MONITORING VALUE GOALS

In Chapter Four, we discussed the fundamental determinants of business value. In most cases the value of an operating business is best measured as a multiple of its earnings or cash flow. And the multiplier to be used is a function of the business's growth

TABLE 5-5
HiGrowth Stores, Inc.

	1982	1983	1984	1985	1986	1987	1988
Revenue	$4,950,000	$4,990,000	$6,150,000	$7,800,000	$9,250,000	$11,700,000	$12,700,000
Cost of sales	4,480,000	4,560,000	5,600,000	6,900,000	8,150,000	10,250,000	11,050,000
Gross profit	470,000	430,000	550,000	900,000	1,100,000	1,450,000	1,650,000
Operating expenses	340,000	360,000	585,000	785,000	950,000	1,380,000	1,540,000
Net income	$ 130,000	$ 70,000	$ (35,000)	$ 115,000	$ 150,000	$ 70,000	$ 110,000
Gross profit margin	9.5%	8.6%	8.9%	11.5%	11.9%	12.4%	13.0%
Operating expenses/revenue	6.9%	7.2%	9.5%	10.1%	10.3%	11.8%	12.1%
Net income/sales	2.6%	1.4%	-0.6%	1.5%	1.6%	0.6%	0.9%
Break-even point with a 1.5% pretax profit margin[*]	$4,362,846	$5,046,283	$7,572,886	$7,817,333	$9,155,398	$12,551,276	$13,319,606
Actual revenue/break-even revenue	113.5%	98.9%	81.2%	99.8%	101.0%	93.2%	95.3%

[*](Operating expenses + 1.5% of revenue)/Gross profit margin.

FIGURE 5–1
HiGrowth Stores, Inc.

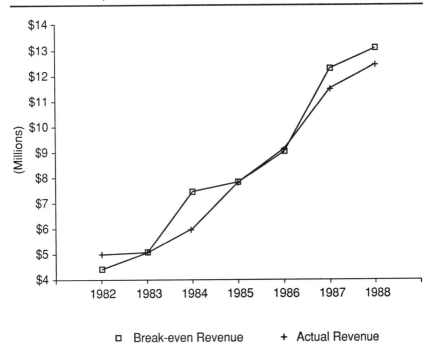

□ Break-even Revenue   + Actual Revenue

rate and the rate of return expected for alternative investments in the market.

Once you have determined the value of your business, you will need to periodically assess how that value is changing over time. The first step is to keep track of annual earnings and cash flow figures, usually adjusted to eliminate one-time events, owner's bonuses, and so forth. If these amounts are not holding steady or are not growing as fast as they were in prior years, then, all other things being equal, the market value of your business is probably not increasing and may be declining.

Second, remember that "all other things" are usually not equal over time either The earnings multiples paid for busi nesses in general or in your particular industry will tend to change with changing conditions in the investment market. Companies that sold for 10 times earnings before the October 1987 stock market decline may have been worth 30 percent less in the months following that crash. It may not seem fair for private companies that are not traded in the market to be so strongly influenced by it. But the fact is that the public markets, for better or worse, tend to act as a benchmark for the value of many private businesses.

Also, the gross sales price of your business is not as important as the net amount of money that you will be able to pocket from the sale after paying taxes. Although income tax rate brackets in general declined after 1986, the rates that apply to the sale of businesses have effectively increased. Two changes have caused this.

First, the capital gains tax that applied to the sale of many businesses or the stock of businesses increased from 20 percent to 28 percent. Therefore, if you had sold a business for a capital gain of $500,000 prior to 1987, you would have netted $400,000 after taxes. But that same transaction would now net the seller only $360,000. Therefore, after the repeal of favorable capital gains tax rates, you would have had to increase the value of your business at least 11 percent just to stay even on an after-tax basis.

A second change in the tax code eliminates the *General Utilities Doctrine* regarding the taxability of the gain from the sale of business assets by a corporation. Before January 1, 1989, most smaller corporations (those worth less than $5 million) that sold their assets and liquidated in a manner specified by the IRS—the preferred method of sale for most private companies—could distribute the proceeds of the sale to the shareholders without having to pay *corporate* income tax on the gain. Only the shareholders would pay tax. Now that situation has changed. The corporation must pay tax on the gain from the sale of its assets. Then only the proceeds remaining after corporate taxes have been paid can be distributed to the shareholders who will pay tax again [!] on the amount they receive. This amounts to a double taxation on the sale of a corporation in which the assets rather than the stock are sold.

As illustrated in Table 5–6, the owner of a corporation worth enough to provide a taxable gain of $500,000 could have netted $400,000 from the sale of that business prior to 1987. But after December 31, 1988, depending on the form of business

TABLE 5–6

	Before 1987 Sale of Assets or Stock	After December 31, 1988	
		Sale of Stock*	Sale of Assets
Profit from sale[+]	$500,000	$500,000	$500,000
Corporate tax due[‡]	0	0	158,250
Net after corporate tax	500,000	500,000	341,750
Shareholder tax due[§]	100,000	140,000	95,690
Net after-tax value	$400,000	$360,000	$246,060
Approximate value required to equal pre-1987 after-tax proceeds		$556,000	$824,000

*Or sale of a qualified S corporation or partnership.

[+]Net proceeds subject to tax.

[‡]In the case of asset sales, this item assumes that the corporation is liquidated in accordance with IRS guidelines. Actual tax is estimated; will vary with particular situations.

[§]Actual tax is estimated; will vary with particular situations.

ownership and the structure of the sale, the same company will net its owner between $246,000 and $360,000. Changes in the tax code have caused the effective after-tax value of some businesses to decrease somewhere between 10 and 39 percent. This decline can be mitigated by methods of sale other than asset sales. But since stock sales tend to be less attractive to buyers of small businesses, this approach may decrease the price anyway.

If you are planning to use the value of your business as the primary source of your retirement income, you must monitor its value from year to year to be sure it will net enough after-tax proceeds to support your retirement. And as tax laws and other changes are announced, you must calculate their impact on your business value so that you can make decisions to help mitigate possible losses.

NONFINANCIAL OBJECTIVES

Although financial objectives are usually the easiest to identify and measure, nonfinancial objectives are important as well. Even when they achieve their financial goals, some business owners become frustrated and discouraged because their businesses in effect become yokes around their owners' necks. Difficult working conditions such as long hours and financial stress can be exciting during a company's start-up phase, but almost everyone will become burned out if such conditions continue indefinitely. Many business owners would do well to consciously substitute some nonfinancial rewards such as flexible hours, long vacations, or community service for maximum financial rewards.

If your business is meeting your financial expectations but does not always provide a satisfactory working environment for you and your employees, then you probably need to consider establishing specific nonfinancial objectives. These objectives should be planned, budgeted, and monitored just like other aspects of your business. They should apply to employees as well as managers and owners. In many cases achieving these so-called nonfinancial objectives can help improve financial rewards as well. Several general categories of nonfinancial goals include

1. *Normal working hours:* The definition of "normal" is naturally an individual consideration. But establish goals and monitor the number of hours worked each week or month.
2. *Vacations:* Schedule and take these on a regular basis. Besides reducing stress, time away from work makes most people more productive when they return.
3. *Reasonable responsibilities:* Delegate appropriate tasks to trained employees. This may be a necessary step before taking regular vacations and working normal hours. It will also usually increase the value of your business by making it less dependent on one or two people.
4. *Working environment:* Even after getting adequate free time, most people spend more time at work than anywhere else. Make sure your working environment is as comfortable and attractive as possible. Set up a process to improve this over time.
5. *Professional development:* Don't become so wrapped up in day-to-day work that you have no time to learn new things about your business or trade. Budget for and schedule professional education and training sessions.

6. *Community service:* Plan appropriate contributions of
either time, money, or business services to public institutions and community service organizations. It is probably better to plan at the beginning of the year and focus
on one or two causes rather than dilute your efforts by
contributing to whatever happens to come up.

SETTING TIME LIMITS

It is usually later than we think when it comes to achieving many goals in life. Establishing financial and nonfinancial
objectives is one thing, but actually achieving them is another.
Every day that a prospective weight loser postpones starting an
exercise program reduces the likelihood of reaching their fitness
goals. And every year that business owners fail to achieve adequate rates of return on their investments decreases their ultimate returns when the time comes to cash in their chips.

Look at Table 5-7 to see the difference between a company that achieves its goals on time and a company that postpones their achievement. In a six-year period Gibraltar Industries made $50,000 a year in free cash flow that the owner was
able to reinvest each year at a 10 percent average annual rate
of return. This amounted to $300,000 over the six-year peri-
od, which compounding annual interest raised to slightly more
than $400,000 by the end of the sixth year.

Flash Industries also generated a total of $300,000 in free
cash during the same six years. But due to lax management
standards Flash actually lost $50,000 in the first three years
and made $150,000 in each of the next three years. Although
Flash's owner ultimately received the same amount of free cash
as Gibraltar's, she was unable to invest anything during the
first three years of operations. She ended up with only about
$330,000, or $70,000 less than the wealth Gibraltar's owner
accumulated because of the compounding annual interest she
lost during the years when no free cash was available.

Failure to meet monthly or annual business objectives *now*,
even if those objectives are eventually achieved, can have a serious negative impact on the total financial success of a business
and its owner

TABLE 5–7
Rate of Return on Reinvestment: 10.0%

	Year					
	1	2	3	4	5	6
Gibraltar Industries						
Annual earnings	$50,000	$ 50,000	$ 50,000	$ 50,000	$ 50,000	$ 50,000
Cumulative earnings	50,000	102,500	160,125	223,256	292,425	368,209
Interest on cumulative earnings	2,500	7,625	13,131	19,169	25,784	33,032
Total equity value	$52,500	$110,125	$173,256	$242,425	$318,209	$401,241
Flash Industries						
Annual earnings	$(50,000)	$ (50,000)	$ (50,000)	$ 50,000	$150,000	$150,000
Cumulative earnings	(50,000)	(100,000)	(150,000)	0	150,000	307,500
Interest on cumulative earnings	0	0	0	0	7,500	22,875
Total equity value	$(50,000)	$(100,000)	$(150,000)	0	$157,500	$330,375

CHAPTER 6

PREPARING TO CASH IN YOUR CHIPS

The journey of a thousand miles may begin with one step, but before that happens you have to decide in which direction to step. You should start thinking now in specific terms about cashing in your chips and extracting all or part of your financial investment from your business. An underlying assumption of this book is that thoughtful business owners don't want to plow money back into their businesses indefinitely. They want to eventually realize reasonable returns from their investments. Deciding when and in what form to realize returns from those investments is essential to operating financially successful businesses.

At the heart of those decisions is your ability to understand and work out a usable exit strategy or ownership transition process for your particular business. *Ownership* in this sense refers to control of business assets and the use of those assets to generate income. "Transition" in the broad sense means removing from your business some or all of its earnings and transferring them directly to yourself to consume or invest in other assets. The ultimate objective for creating a business that cannot continue profitable growth indefinitely, which means virtually any private company, is to carry out an exit strategy that provides the greatest net benefit to the owners.

HAVING THE CORRECT
OWNERSHIP STRUCTURE

The ideal time to start thinking about your exit strategy and ownership transition process is right when you begin the business. By thinking in the start-up phase about how and in what form you will eventually take funds out of your business, you will find it easier to make correct decisions, or at least avoid making extremely bad ones. It is never too early, and with any luck it is not yet too late, to organize the operations and structure of your business in a manner that provides the greatest flexibility and most favorable conditions for transferring earnings out of your company.

One key decision that is typically made right when the business begins is the form of ownership. Most business owners make, or stumble into, this decision without thinking through its impact on their eventual withdrawal of funds. But even if you initially made a decision that was the best one under your original circumstances, you will need to reevaluate it frequently. Both your business objectives and important outside factors such as the income tax code change over time. All three basic forms of business ownership—sole proprietorship, partnership, and corporation—may be appropriate at various points in your business's life. Being in the right form at the right time requires considerable initial planning as well as some educated guesses about what might happen in the future.

In order to make the best decision regarding ownership structure, you'll need to make some basic forecasts or assumptions about the potential timing and form of your business earnings. The basic earnings patterns that your business may experience include

- Expected losses followed by positive cash flow and general growth over time.
- Expected losses followed by positive cash flow but not much growth.
- Profitable operations and a growth rate that requires retaining substantial earnings for reinvestment.

- Profitable operations and a growth rate that does not require retaining substantial earnings for reinvestment.
- Profitable operations that decline in volume over time.
- Declining business volume that becomes unprofitable.

In most businesses it is not easy to accurately predict which of these earnings conditions will occur at particular moments in the future. But you need to make the best possible estimate as to which earnings pattern will likely occur during the next one to five years. Then use that earnings estimate as a basis for selecting the best business structure to meet your objectives during that time.

You'll need to remember two major points about selecting a business structure that will maximize your income as a business owner. First, selecting a business structure generally involves trade-offs that make it nearly impossible to have the best possible structure under all expected circumstances. For example, it may be a good idea to have a standard corporation (referred to in the IRS Code as a *C corporation*) to minimize income taxes during the time you need to plow all your firm's earnings back into your company to support growing operations or repay debts. This structure would help shelter business earnings of less than $75,000 at relatively low corporate tax rates, thus making more money available for additional investment or debt service. But if you are planning to transfer the ownership of your business by a sale of assets during the next few years, then the standard corporation structure may cause stockholders to suffer double taxation on profits from the sale. Therefore, to maximize return on investment, you must consider the entire life cycle of your business before committing to an ownership structure.

Second, fluctuating business conditions, new tax laws, and a business owner's changing plans and expectations can make an initially correct ownership structure obsolete. Be sure to check regularly with your legal and tax advisers to be sure you don't need to make changes in ownership structure to maximize the financial benefits that you will eventually receive from your company.

The main factors that influence business ownership structure are listed in Table 6–1 along with the most likely options

TABLE 6-1

Basic Possible Conditions Affecting Ownership Structure

1.	Number of owners now	1	2 or more closely related	2 or more unrelated

1. Number of owners now	1	2 or more closely related	2 or more unrelated
Possible ownership structure	S, C, SC	P, C, SC	P, C, SC
2. Expected earnings during next 1–2 years	Losses	Earnings less than reinvestment requirements	Earnings exceed reinvestment requirements
Possible ownership structure	S, P, SC	C	S, P, SC
3. Current earnings or expected earnings after 1–2 years	Earnings less than reinvestment requirements	Earnings exceed reinvestment requirements	Earnings exceed reinvestment requirements
Possible ownership structure	C	S, P, SC	S, P, SC
4. Primary source of earnings	Ongoing operations	Asset appreciation	Increase in value of operations
Possible ownership structure	S, P, C, SC	S, P, SC	S, P, C, SC
5. Likely owners when current owner is inactive	Family member	Nonrelated co-owner employee or outside party	
Possible ownership structure	P, C, SC	P, C, SC	
6. Number of owners in the future	1	2 or more closely related	2 or more unrelated
Possible ownership structure	S, C, SC	P, C, SC	P, C, SC
7. Probable means of ownership transfer	Gift	Sale of assets	Sale of stock
Possible ownership structure	P, C, SC	S, P, SC	P, C, SC

S = Sole proprietorship
P = Partnership
C = Corporation
SC = S Corporation

for each condition. By checking the conditions that apply to your present situation, you can determine which ownership options are presently suitable. Then by checking the conditions that you think will exist as your business changes, you can see which ownership structure will be best in the future. If the ownership structure you have today is likely to be inappropriate in the future, then then you can make plans to change it or at least minimize its adverse effects.

ELEMENTS OF THE EXIT STRATEGY PLAN

An exit strategy is the means by which you intend to withdraw investments from your business or otherwise remove yourself from active management. Creating an exit strategy plan involves thinking through exactly how you will convert your business investment into liquid assets that you can consume or invest elsewhere, or how you will pass the ownership of your business to a family member for continued operation. An exit strategy or ownership transition plan has four basic elements.

1. *Establishing the basic objective:* Like everyone else, you must eventually cease being active in your business; at that time you will have only two basic options. First, you can withdraw your financial investment from the company either gradually over time or in a complete sale. Or, second, you can keep your company intact to transfer to your children or other beneficiaries. If your company is highly successful, you can choose to withdraw only current income (e.g., dividends) to live on in retirement while passing on the basic business intact.

2. *Selecting a strategy:* Once you have selected your basic objective, you must lay out a strategy for achieving it. Figure 6–1 charts most of the options available for meeting whatever objective you choose.

If you plan to sell your business either to family members or nonfamily parties, then you will be withdrawing your capital from the business. Will you do it piecemeal over time, in one fell swoop of a sale, or in some combination of the two?

If you are going to pass your business intact to family members rather than sell it, you have two basic questions to

FIGURE 6–1

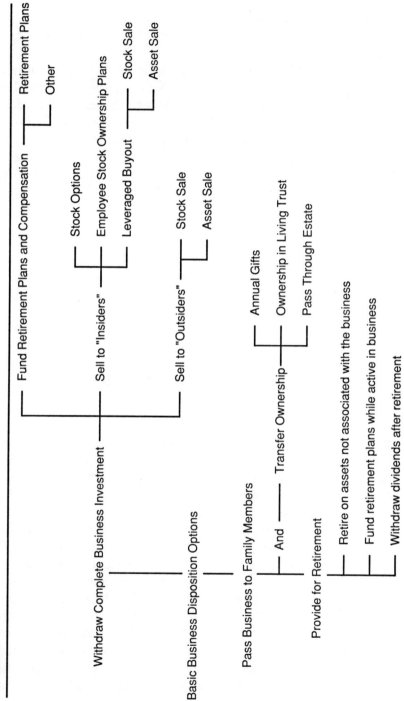

answer. How will you meet your financial needs for retirement income? And what method will you choose to pass ownership to your heirs?

3. *Timing:* It is critical to establish a schedule for implementing your transition strategy. Nothing seems more absurd than the tendency of business owners to spend 10, 20, or even 40 years establishing and operating a company and then try to sell it in a few weeks with no prior planning or provision for retirement income. By laying out your plan *now* and establishing dates for achieving each step, you will make sure that you end up where you want to be. You will also have time to take corrective action in the event of unforeseen developments or changes in your objectives.

4. *Monitoring and reevaluation:* Once you have established your strategy, implementation plan, and timetable you must periodically monitor their progress. Too often business owners say that they have "solved" their transition- planning issues because several years ago they wrote a buy-sell agreement with their partners or worked out an estate plan with their lawyer. In most cases those agreements and plans gather dust, and nobody can really remember what they actually say much less if they are relevant to the business situation today.

Several years ago I was a trustee for an estate in which one of the primary assets was stock in a private company. Many years before, the three stockholders of the company had drawn up a buy-sell agreement providing that the company or its shareholders would purchase the stock from each shareholder's estate in the event of a shareholder's death. The agreement specified that the value of the stock in the deceased shareholder's estate would be determined by a particular formula that measured asset value as of the date of death. The company was obligated to pay cash for the stock in each shareholder's estate. And if sufficient funds were unavailable within the company, the remaining shareholders were obligated to buy the stock. At the time of the agreement the valuation formula may have made sense to the shareholders, and the company was generating enough cash to easily purchase the stock. The agreement seemed to be a great method to provide money to the stockholders' heirs, and the business owners were confident they had solved their transition-planning and estate issues.

During the years after the agreement was written, the nature and earnings of the company changed profoundly. Nobody thought to change the buy-sell agreement accordingly. When the first of the stockholders, who owned 20 percent of the company's stock, passed away, the buy-sell agreement in his estate was dusted off. It turned out that the valuation formula developed many years before required the company to pay the deceased stockholder's estate an amount equal to about one-half the current value of the entire company. Since the business was not in a position to make the required payments, the remaining shareholders were personally liable for the difference. This was a wonderful windfall for the estate of the first shareholder who passed away, but it turned out to be a disaster for the remaining stockholders and their families! As you can imagine, after paying off the first shareholder's estate, the remaining stockholders changed their buy-sell agreement to reflect the current condition of the business.

WHY BUSINESS OWNERS FAIL TO HAVE A VIABLE EXIT STRATEGY

Many business owners fail to acknowledge that the way they are operating their businesses will not achieve their financial and personal objectives. By not setting explicit objectives and a timetable for achieving them, they are almost assured of being disappointed with the results. But once they commit to and track progress toward specific results, their chances of being successful improve.

Business owners typically fail to plan adequately for their retirement and the ultimate disposition of their businesses for several reasons. First, they find it difficult to acknowledge their own mortality. They don't want to admit that they will not always be able to carry out the work they have done all their lives. Second, ownership transition involves giving up control of a business that in many cases has been run as a little kingdom in which the business owner has no need to explain or apologize for any actions. Owners like these tend to think nobody else can make decisions or deal with customers and employees as well as they can. So they delay relinquishing control or even thinking about doing so.

I think there is also a third major reason that business owners of all ages and attitudes fail to make and carry out effective, profitable business plans and exit strategies. They are unwilling to accept the fundamental economic reality that all resources are limited. The time, money, and management abilities of even the largest, most successful companies are limited. And those limits are much lower still for small companies. Yet people's imaginations and desires are unlimited. They resist accepting that their business and personal options are finite and that over time those options tend to become even more limited. Although there may be some heroic exceptions, most business owners let their companies drift into a comfort level of earnings performance that after a while is difficult to rise above. In many cases the profits earned at that comfort level are insufficient to meet the owner's ultimate financial goals. This fact is usually unpleasant to discover in the process of making specific plans for a business exit strategy. Therefore, rather than face the world of limited resources, many business owners find it more comfortable in the short run to avoid thinking about their ultimate goals.

A while ago the owner of a professional practice came to me for advice on a particular business problem involving her current operations. The business paid its owner a six-figure annual salary, all of which she consumed each year because of her lifestyle. Since the business had little resale value, none of the current business earnings were being set aside for investment, and the owner was more than 60 years old, I asked how she intended to support herself in retirement. Her response was that years ago she had purchased the building in which the business was conducted and had always intended to sell it and retire on the proceeds. The problem with this strategy was that the net after-tax proceeds of the property sale would be about $250,000. Investing that money in relatively safe assets that would provide income over the owner's projected life expectancy could provide only about $20,000 to $25,000 of pretax annual income. This relatively small amount plus social security would hardly provide for the active, affluent lifestyle to which this business owner is accustomed! So although the business owner had an exit strategy, she had never bothered to quantify it and find out that it simply didn't work in the real world.

GENERIC APPROACHES TO TRANSITION

Although the task of establishing business exit and transition plans is complex and somewhat intimidating to most people, there are really only a few basic, or generic, options from which to choose. Once you have assessed your business situation and long-term objectives, you should be able to focus on the most feasible options and not become confused by too many alternatives and "what ifs." A key ingredient in successful planning for all kinds of business issues is to determine up front which options are impossible or unlikely to apply to your circumstances. Then you can devote your limited resources to doing the best possible job with the workable alternatives.

A careful review of Figure 6–1 will show that some of these options are mutually exclusive. Once you decide that a particular course of action is inappropriate, you can concentrate on the options that best meet your objectives. Even if some options can be simultaneously carried out, you will likely discover that you really have too few resources, such as time and money, to carry out more than one. And by quantifying the likely outcome of each feasible option, you may find that one has a considerable financial advantage over the others.

As a private business owner, your first decision must be whether to pass your company on—that is, give it—to members of your family. If you decide to give complete ownership to family members. Figure 6–1 provides some ideas and Chapter 7, Creating a Dynasty, discusses them more completely.

If on the other hand you decide not to give a substantial portion of your business to family members, then you have in effect decided to withdraw your investment from the company. There are several reasons to choose this option. In many cases there is no suitable or willing family member to pass the business on to. Clearly the only option then is to sell the business in one form or another.

Even when business owners have a suitable heir, they and their children assume, often without justification, that passing it on is the only natural or appropriate thing to do. But a family company may provide too little surplus cash to fund the current owner's retirement. Or perhaps no suitable arrangements have been made for estate taxes or other considerations. Then it may be necessary to sell the business either to a family member or to someone else at market price and terms. In place of or in addition to selling the business, an owner may be able to withdraw a large part of her or his investment under favorable tax conditions through profit-sharing and retirement benefit plans. These possibilities are discussed in Chapter 8.

CHAPTER 7

CREATING
A DYNASTY

Many Americans think that the ultimate expression of entrepreneurial success is to create a great family dynasty such as
those founded by the Rockefellers, Fords, Pillsburys, or the
fictional Ewings of Dallas. And family business owners who
never come close to creating national or even regional corporations often aspire to start their own dynasties on a local scale.
The unspoken motivation for many business owners is probably to create an entity that extends beyond the life span of its
founder. It is no coincidence that many entrepreneurs refer to
their businesses as their "baby." Despite the professed desire
of many business founders to pass on their companies or professional practices to children, in-laws, or other relatives, it is
estimated that no more than about 30 percent of all private
companies survive into a second generation of ownership.

In many cases nobody in the family is available to carry
on the business. Perhaps there are no children, or the children
who are available may have no interest in the family business.
Even if you have children or in-laws who want to take over your
family company, you have no guarantee that they are qualified
to do so. Warren Buffett, Chairman of Berkshire Hathaway, has
reportedly observed,

> Would anyone say the best way to pick a championship Olympic
> team is to select the sons and daughters of those who won 20
> years ago? Giving someone a favored position just because his
> old man accomplished something is a crazy way for a society to
> compete

Your children probably have many talents, skills, and positive personality traits. But that does not automatically mean they should eventually take over your business. And even if they are potentially suitable owners and managers, it still takes planning and hard work on everyone's part to make family ownership transition work.

PREPARING FOR THE FAMILY TO TAKE OVER

Assuming suitable family members are waiting in the wings to take over your company, how do you go about doing it? Given the complex financial and emotional issues involved, there can be no simple answer. You are unlikely to establish a satisfactory succession plan by thinking about the problem for just a few hours or days. On the contrary, if you want satisfactory results, you'll need to develop a multistep process involving several parties over a significant period of time.

The first step is to identify everyone who needs to be involved in the business succession process. This means more than just the one family member you assume will take over from you. Every family business has a number of *stakeholders* and other involved parties to consider and consult if the succession process is going to be successful. The most obvious involved parties are you and the members of your family. Be sure that all family members are included in the planning process even if you do not think they will be actively involved in your business. It's important to confirm early on that you understand everyone's motivations and expectations.

Besides your family, other important stakeholders include nonfamily managers and key employees, other employees, and perhaps major suppliers or customers. These people have very definite interests in what your family plans to do with the business. The nonfamily members will want to know what the ground rules are for family members working at your firm and where they can fit into the company over the long haul. The more uncertainty or perceived unfairness and irrationality regarding family versus nonfamily employees, the more difficult it will be to retain good employees. That in turn will make it more difficult for your company to be as financially successful as it might be. Depending on the nature of your business, you may also need to consider important suppliers or customers in your family succession plans. When these outside parties are aware of your succession plans and think that the results are workable, they will feel more secure about established relationships, policies, and services continuing beyond your current ownership.

Depending on the size, value, and complexity of your business, you will also want to involve experienced attorneys, CPAs, bankers, insurance brokers, investment counselors, and other business advisers. Outside advisers can play several valuable roles. First, one or more of them can act as impartial associates to facilitate the entire process. The successful succession-planning process will probably be long and difficult. Like all long and difficult aspects of business ownership, this tends to be put off indefinitely unless someone is given responsibility to make it happen. Also, a trusted and respected outsider who has no financial or emotional interest in the results of the succession plan can bring a fair and impartial perspective to thorny issues. A good professional facilitator can coordinate the roles of other outside professionals and help everyone achieve acceptable results for both the company and the family. You will need to establish a budget for both the time and money to be allotted to this process just as you would for any business investment.

Once you have identified the stakeholders and outside advisers, you can begin working on the succession plan. First rough out your thoughts on all the major issues, using your facilitator or other advisers for additional ideas and assistance. Then involve each appropriate party in discussing and understanding the issues that directly affect them. Finally, once you have established your succession plan, document and share the final results with all your family members and stakeholders.

You may have found that many business planning processes are too abstract and drawn-out to be practical for small companies like yours. To make this succession process relatively painless, try preparing a written answer to each of the following questions:

1. What is your timetable for exiting from day-to-day operations, and who will take over each of the tasks you now
   perform?
2. What are the policies for employing family members?
3. Who are the designated successors for management of
   the business?
4. What will be the role for family members who are not
   active in the business?
5. What is your basic strategy for passing on the business
   ownership?
6. What will be the decision-making process for ownership
   issues?
7. What will be the decision-making process for operations?
8. Is it necessary to have key managers who are not family
   members?
9. How will you support your personal retirement after
   becoming inactive in the business?

If you tackle one of these questions every week or month, you
will soon have a complete plan.

ELEMENTS OF THE SUCCESSION PLAN

What Is Your Timetable for Exiting from Day-to-Day Operations, and Who Will Take Over Each of the Tasks You Perform?
Decide on specific dates when you will withdraw from active
responsibility for certain aspects of running your company.
Then announce when you will delegate these tasks to family
members or other employees and tell them what they have to
do to prepare to take over those responsibilities. This phased
withdrawal can give your heirs an opportunity to develop skills
and confidence without making major mistakes.

You will never successfully withdraw from your family
business if you refuse to delegate important tasks to well-
trained and motivated successors. Remember to delegate *both*
the responsibility and the authority. Act as a coach, but fight
the temptation to second-guess every minor decision. As you
delegate more day-to-day tasks, you should be able to assume

more of the classic role of chief executive. You can become a manager who establishes overall direction and vision for the business while indirectly monitoring operations through subordinate managers.

What Are the Policies for Employing Family Members?

Decide how family members will be hired, evaluated, compensated, and promoted. Then let the family members and appropriate nonfamily employees know what the standards and expectations are. The best approach is to provide descriptions of responsibilities, requirements, and compensation for each position in your company. Fill those positions with family members only when they meet the stated requirements. If you implement this policy, you will be better assured that your heir-apparent is qualified to run the business when the time comes. And nonfamily members will have more confidence in and respect for family employees.

Many business owners make it a point of pride to have their children start in relatively menial positions and then work their way up to the management level. Depending on the nature of your business, this can be effective. But in many cases children join the family business because it is easier than getting a good education or gaining greater experience at another company. Small businesses already tend to become inbred and miss out on new ideas when too many of their employees have worked most of their careers there. While working their way up to management, your children can gain a good knowledge of the details of the business, but they may not necessarily obtain the broader business knowledge and insights needed to effectively operate a company in the late 20th-century American economy. Lacking this broader background, they may be unable to guide your company to future success. Eventually your business may start moving backward as the conditions that allowed success in the last generation no longer exist.

A 1986 survey by the Laventhol & Horwath accounting firm indicated that 65 percent of business owners thought their children should acquire experience with another company before coming to work at the family business. Only 11 percent of those surveyed thought their children should join the family firm right out of school.

Who Are the Designated Successors for Management of the Business?

To answer this question, you must consider both family and nonfamily employees. Depending on its size, your business may have more management positions than available and qualified family members can fill. In this case, you'll need to decide which positions to fill with your family members and train them accordingly. You can then select and train nonfamily members for any remaining positions and give them the necessary incentive to remain with your business.

Let people know as soon as possible who the designated future company leaders are. It may be difficult to tell one or more of your children that you do not consider them appropriate to eventually run your company. But at least by putting this issue on the table early, you will give them a chance to develop interests and opportunities outside your family's business if they aspire to do so.

What Will Be the Role for Family Members Who Are Not Active in the Business?

You may have family members who are not active in the business as employees. If so, you must clarify what role, if any, you plan for them to have in your company. If you intend to let them inherit an ownership interest in your business, then you must determine what involvement and benefits they will have as owners. You will have to make specific provisions to enforce your intentions. Family members who are active in a business commonly tend to develop conflicts of interest and differences with their inactive relatives. If possible it is usually best to leave assets other than an interest in a closely held business to people who are not active in that business. This will go a long way toward heading off prospective disputes between management and stockholders.

If you want inactive family members to retain substantial ownership interests, you may want to create a specific class of stock, say a convertible preferred stock, that they will inherit. A preferred stock will guarantee them some dividend income from the company as long as it is successful. And if it is convertible to common stock, your heirs will be able to take advantage of any future appreciation in the value of the business that may be realized through increased profitability and eventual sale.

You may also want to make some specific provisions that will allow inactive stockholders to sell their stock back to the company at a value that is fair to them but also affordable to the company. This can be accomplished by having a buy-sell agreement among the shareholders or between the shareholders and the company. The details of such an agreement must be carefully thought out if they are going to meet your specific concerns. Be wary of the "canned" or "boilerplate" stockholder agreements attorneys sometimes present.

What Is Your Basic Strategy for Passing On the Business Ownership within Your Family?

If you want some member of your family to own your company after you are no longer active in the business or even alive, who should it be and what form of ownership would be best? If you have only one prospective heir, then determining how to pass the company to its ultimate owner is relatively simple. But if you have more than one prospective heir the problem becomes more complex.

You need to explicitly determine whether all your heirs will end up owning part of the business or not. The practice in many families is for the original business owner to will equal amounts of stock to all his or her heirs. This method seems intuitively fair and is relatively simple, but it frequently has unanticipated negative results for both family members and the business.

For example, some family members may be active in the business while others are not. The active members tend to regard the company as solely theirs and want to keep operational control and all or most ownership benefits for themselves and their immediate families. If this happens and the inactive family members accept the results, then their inheritance will have little or no value. And if the inactive family members don't accept the results and decide to challenge the distribution of ownership benefits, the ensuing struggle can destroy the company or cause its sale to someone outside the family. Is either one of these situations desirable?

One of the most visible and colorful recent examples of this worst of all possible worlds was the situation that befell the Bingham family and their ownership of the *Louisville Courier-Journal* newspaper. Bingham family members who were active in the company would not let their inactive siblings participate fully in management or receive significant income from their ownership interests. The inactive family stockholders sued for fair treatment and ultimately the only way to satisfy the inactive shareholders' interests was to sell control of the company to outsiders. The practical result was the instant demise of an American business dynasty.

The three basic ways to pass ownership interest to your family are (1) to give it away while you are still alive, (2) to pass it to others from your estate, or (3) to sell it to family members. One of the important considerations in deciding on one of these options is the value of your business and your taxable estate. Under present law the assets in your estate will eventually be subject to federal taxes to the extent that their value exceeds $600,000.

If you intend to have family members own your business after your death, then it may be a good idea to begin giving away some of that ownership now. The portion of your business's value that you give away now will not be taxed in your estate. Therefore, you may be able to avoid a significant amount of potential estate taxes by starting an early gift program. Generally the tax laws allow anyone to give $10,000 each year to an individual without having to recognize gift or income taxes.

For example, assume you and your spouse own a business that is appraised for tax purposes at $1 million and it is no longer increasing in value. If you want four people to end up owning the business, say two children and their spouses, you and your spouse could give a total of $80,000 worth of stock each year to your eventual heirs. While it would take 13 years to give away the entire company, which may or may not be practical or even necessary, an active gifting program would still allow you to give away a substantial portion of your taxable estate. It is extremely important that the value you claim for the gifts can be substantiated if it is ever questioned by the IRS. Otherwise the IRS may come back later and charge gift taxes plus interest and penalties that could more than negate the estate tax savings.

Any portion of your business's value that you do not give away to your family will end up in your or your spouse's estate. This may cause problems for your heirs, who will have to pay estate taxes on a highly illiquid asset. The most effective way to minimize estate taxes is to get timely professional advice that will help keep as much of your business as possible from ever becoming susceptible to them. This process is becoming increasingly difficult as tax authorities respond to the clever strategies of tax lawyers and CPAs. Unfortunately the highly effective estate tax minimization schemes known as recapitalizations or business freezes are now specifically prohibited. But other options may be available, depending on your particular circumstances.

One approach is to create a trust that owns the stock of your business while you are still alive. Although the trust owns the stock, you can still arrange to control and receive income from the assets as long as you are alive. After your death your heirs can become the owners or beneficiaries of the trust. By putting your business assets into a trust now, you may be able to avoid some probate costs associated with your estate's value. Current federal law taxes the value of estates in excess of $600,000. You and your spouse can each put your respective ownership interests into separate trusts whose ultimate beneficiaries are your children. Each trust could take advantage of the $600,000 exclusion and potentially shelter up to $1.2 million from estate tax.

Under some circumstances, the estate tax on a family business whose value is a large enough percentage of the owner's total assets can be remitted to the IRS in time payments that are subject to interest. In effect the tax becomes a liability of the business. But this option is not available in many situations because the specific facts of the estate do not allow for time payments under IRS rules. And even if such payment is allowed, your company will be saddled with a large debt that will depress profitability for many years and perhaps prevent it from making the investments needed to remain competitive.

After you have done everything possible to minimize the portion of your business's value that will be left in your estate, you can fund any remaining tax liability with life insurance or other money that you earmark for this purpose in a *sinking fund*. Starting early with life insurance payments may be the most practical approach, and this method can protect your family from onerous estate taxes in the event of your untimely death. Two common pitfalls in the insurance method are buying too much or not buying enough. When you buy insurance to cover estate taxes on a closely held business, you should have an independent appraiser estimate your business's value. Insurance salespeople are usually not qualified to do the appraisal and may tend to overvalue your company because they would like to sell a larger policy. You should also ensure that your insurance coverage keeps up with increases in the taxable value of your company so your family and estate are not exposed to unplanned tax liabilities.

Unless you plan early enough, you may find no easy way to avoid or minimize estate taxes on your business. In many instances, lack of prior funding and planning has caused businesses to be sold outside the family, sometimes at distress prices, to meet IRS obligations.

Once you have provided for taxes on the portion of your estate in excess of $600,000, you can arrange to have the stock from your estate distributed directly to your designated heirs or have it held in a trust for their benefit. A trust that holds and controls your company's stock can help prevent ownership control from becoming increasingly fragmented over time as more heirs become owners. If you wish, the trust can be fully or partially managed by independent professionals with the fiduciary responsibility of looking after the interests of your beneficiaries who may not be qualified to look after their own interests.

If you distribute stock directly to your beneficiaries, you can retain some control of the stock by means of a stockholder agreement governing all the shareholders or by the conditions of the trust. For example, you may want to create buy-sell restrictions that prevent sale of the stock to nonfamily members, require dividends for stockholders so that inactive stockholders can benefit from their ownership, or have special voting requirements for selecting directors or making major decisions.

In some instances you may want your heirs to have the family business but do not want to give it to them. Once you have determined the value of your business, selling to family members is not materially different from selling to nonfamily members. As a seller, you will of course have to pay income tax on any gain you make from the sale. If you sell the business to a family member for less than its fair market value, the IRS may contend that you owe a gift tax on the difference between the company's fair value and the amount you actually received.

It may not be practical or desirable to give your entire business to prospective heirs. For one thing, you may need to receive the value of the business to fund your retirement. Selling your business to your heirs at a fair value while you are still relatively young has the additional advantage of removing from your estate any appreciation in the business that occurs after the sale. This approach may effectively freeze your estate value, although you will still have to pay current income taxes on your gain from the sale, and any of the value you receive from the sale that you don't eventually spend may end up being taxed in your estate.

You can, however, effectively freeze the value of your estate without leaving any taxable asset by selling your company to your heirs in exchange for an annuity payment that ceases upon your death or the death of your spouse, whichever is later. Such an annuity could be purchased from a life insurance company or other source. This transaction must meet the specific requirements of the tax code. This annuity would provide a fixed amount of annual income for the rest of your life, and its value would be based on your life expectancy at the date of the sale. To avoid creating a taxable gift, the present value of the annuity, based on discounted cash flow, must equal the market value of your business. The beauty of this arrangement from an estate-planning perspective is that the annuity will leave no taxable value in your or your spouse's estate since the payments cease upon death. The family members who buy the business are therefore essentially purchasing your company at its current value on a long-term contract. The cost of the purchase will be greater if you live longer than the life expectancy tables calculate, but this cost should be offset by the potential benefit of estate tax reduction. Finally, the annuity created from the business sale can be used to fund your retirement. A drawback to this approach is that the exchange of your stock for the annuity will probably be taxed at the time of the transaction rather than as you receive the funds.

How Will You Support Your Personal Retirement after Becoming Inactive in the Business?

Even though you want to keep the business in the family, you must still provide enough income to support your retirement. One method is to put aside excess profits over the years into profit-sharing and pension programs that will be fully funded by the time you are ready to retire. To do this, you can use your company's pretax earnings, thereby creating a tax shelter as well as an investment program. By setting up and funding this program over a number of years, you may be able to create a sufficient retirement nest egg. That way your family business will not have to support you out of its earnings after it no longer employs you. But if you have not already made provision for your retirement, then you will have to continue receiving income from your company after you retire. You can do this in several ways.

If you remain somewhat active in the company, then you can receive consulting fees or director's fees. These would be tax deductible to the company but would be subject to payment by you of both income and social security taxes. As shown in part A of Table 7–1, the cost to your company of distributing $50,000 per year in compensation to you in this manner effectively declines as your company's average tax rate increases.

Another possible source of income would be payments for use of property or equipment that you own and the company leases from you. These leases need to be at reasonable market rates to pass IRS muster, but that does not prevent them from being on the high side of a reasonable range. Again assume

TABLE 7–1
Net Cost of Compensation to Owner in the Form of Salary, Rental Income, and Dividends at Various Corporate Tax Rates

	Average Corporate Tax Rate on Owner's Compensation			
	15.0%	20.0%	29.5%	34.0%
A.				
Salary, consulting, or director's fee	$50,000	$50,000	$50,000	$50,000
Company payroll taxes	3,600	3,600	3,600	3,600
Tax deductions	(8,040)	(10,720)	(15,812)	(18,224)
Net paid by company	$45,560	$42,880	$37,788	$35,376
Owner's income	$50,000	$50,000	$50,000	$50,000
Owner's social security taxes	3,375	3,375	3,375	3,375
Net pre–income tax amount	$46,625	$46,625	$46,625	$46,625
B.				
Rent to owner	$50,000	$50,000	$50,000	$50,000
Company payroll taxes				
Tax deductions	(7,500)	(10,000)	(14,750)	(17,000)
Net paid by company	$42,500	$40,000	$35,250	$33,000
Owner's income	$50,000	$50,000	$50,000	$50,000
Owner's social security taxes				
Net pre–income tax amount	$50,000	$50,000	$50,000	$50,000
C.				
Dividend to owner	$50,000	$50,000	$50,000	$50,000
Company payroll taxes				
Tax deductions				
Net paid by company	$50,000	$50,000	$50,000	$50,000
Owner's income	$50,000	$50,000	$50,000	$50,000
Owner's social security taxes				
Net pre–income tax amount	$50,000	$50,000	$50,000	$50,000

that you want $50,000 per year in compensation and that you own property with an annual rental value equal to about that much. The net cost to your company of renting the property declines as your company's average tax rate increases. This approach delivers the most value to you at the least cost to your company since payment and income for rental property are not subject to payroll and social security tax withholding. The property you are leasing to your company may also provide some personal tax deductions to partially offset the income you receive. Your annual rental payments can be scheduled to increase along with inflation or other cost increases. The obvious hitch to this approach is that you will need to have the foresight and financial means to pay for the property before you are ready to retire.

Owners of small private companies typically avoid taking dividends because they are not tax-deductible to the company. As shown in part C of Table 7–1, it will cost your company more to provide your $50,000 annual income by dividends than by other methods. But the net cost difference between dividends and salary for this amount after payroll taxes is not really that much for corporations in low tax brackets. And some fairly profitable corporations can stay in those low brackets if they have deductions for employee stock ownership plans or have large depreciation write-offs due to equipment investments. Despite their possible tax costs, dividends can provide a clean and simple way for you to receive some additional retirement income.

What Will Be the Decision-Making Process for Ownership Issues?

Remember that ownership does not have to be equated with operational management. Just because substantial shareholders aren't employed by a company doesn't mean they shouldn't have some say in major business decisions. You can do this by giving them representation on a board of directors or putting special provisions into the company's by-laws that require their involvement on particular decisions. Again, remember the ever-present likelihood that people's needs and interests in the ownership of a closely held business will diverge over time. It may be important to draft creative stockholder agreements that prevent inevitable differences of opinion from destroying your company or family.

One of the most common areas of disagreement on ownership issues is whether or not the business should be sold to someone outside the family. This question typically arises when inactive shareholders decide they are not getting any current financial return from their stock in the form of dividends. When the unhappy shareholders want to sell their stock, other shareholders will often fail to pay fair value. One way to resolve this issue is to make all the stockholders subject to a buy-sell agreement that includes a *shotgun clause*. This kind of agreement requires that if one shareholder (the buyer) makes an offer for the stock of another shareholder (the seller) or locates a buyer who will make an offer, the seller must either agree to the sale or purchase the ownership interest of the initial buyer for the price and terms originally offered. This type of agreement prevents buyers from making unfair or "lowball" offers since they would be obligated to sell their stock to their co-owners for the same price and terms. Assuming that all the parties have roughly the same ability to locate qualified buyers or raise money to purchase other parties' stock, nobody should be tempted to take unfair advantage of their fellow share-holders.

What Will Be the Decision-Making Process for Operations?

Even if all your family members can agree on major ownership issues and policies, you still have to set up a method to carry out day-to-day operating decisions. If you are succeeded by a single manager, this problem will resolve itself once you stop running the show. But serious problems can develop if more than one family member, or a combination of family members and other managers, are left to run the business.

From a business point of view the easiest and most effective course of action is probably to designate one heir to be in charge. To give your business the greatest possible chance of success, you'll need to select that person on the basis of background and demonstrated ability rather than simply age, sex, or number of years in the business. Although this solution is typically the most logical, it may not always seem fair to other family members who aspire to lead, or at least remain equal to, their siblings. For the sake of family harmony, then, you may decide to avoid choosing a single chief executive.

In place of a single designated leader, some business owners transfer senior management responsibilities to two or more of their heirs who function as an executive team or committee. The idea is that a collegial group with shared authority will provide a diversity of perspectives combined with a willingness to reach decisions by consensus. This approach is also designed to placate sibling rivalries. But such a method is unlikely to work unless all the coexecutives have comparable business and personal communications skills and are already used to making effective decisions as a group. As a practical matter such ideal circumstances virtually never exist. If executive committees are such a good way to run day-to-day business operations, why aren't more public companies, which are presumably more complex than most family businesses, run that way? Probably because consensus decision making doesn't tend to work well in either emergencies, which require rapid, controlled action, or in the sort of visionary management needed to take advantage of changing markets and opportunities. Therefore, all other things being equal, I think committee-run companies are more likely to fail or at least decline in a dynamic market economy.

Is It Necessary to Have Key Managers Who Are Not Family Members?

In all but the smallest family-owned companies, you will have to develop a strategy for bringing in and retaining nonfamily managers or key employees. Seldom are there enough qualified heirs to fill all the key positions in a multidepartment or multibusiness company. Nonfamily managers and key employees have to be compensated and provided benefits and opportunities comparable to those they can get elsewhere. Otherwise your business will be harmed by its inability to hire and retain the talent it needs to be profitable and to grow.

In theory it should be no more difficult to find good people to work in family-owned businesses than in larger companies. Not many workers and managers in our economy actually obtain significant ownership interests in the companies they work for, and only a few people ever reach the most senior management levels. Therefore, the fact that a nonfamily member will never have ownership or chief executive authority in a family business should not in itself prevent your company from retaining top-class talent. But several factors typical of family companies may tend to keep top people from wanting to work for and stay with your company. High-quality professional people do not want to work in a company where senior management decisions appear to be made in arbitrary, nonbusinesslike ways. If family dynamics lead to poor-quality decision making or lack of decision making in a company, good employees will come to resent family members' involvement.

Also, business owners and their families are usually willing to defer income and work long hours because they expect to reap long-term benefits from their ownership that offset their sacrifices. But it is unreasonable to expect people who will never have the benefits of ownership to make such personal and economic sacrifices. They must receive enough compensation to eliminate any opportunity cost they might incur by forgoing jobs in larger organizations that typically offer extensive benefits and retirement programs. Therefore, if you want to keep the kind of talent required to be successful and profitable you may need to set up compensation systems that motivate important nonfamily employees to remain for the long haul and do their best work. Sometimes that means they will be better compensated than family members, especially during financially difficult times in your business.

WRITE IT DOWN AND USE IT

After answering these succession questions and making the best possible decisions on the various issues, you should have your tax and legal advisers document your decisions in the proper legal and tax formats. Your intentions may be the best, but unless the transition documents are drawn up and kept current with the tax code and your family's needs, your business's future is unlikely to unfold as you would wish. Once your succession plan is complete, you can withdraw from active ownership of your business or, upon your death, pass your business along to your heirs in a way that benefits your family and allows the company to remain in the family for another generation.

In most cases, if you don't take care to document a succession plan, the *best* that can happen is that your family members will be confused about their responsibilities and will incur unnecessary costs in dealing with that confusion. The worst that can, and frequently does, happen is that your business and family will have to shoulder huge tax, legal, and other costs to straighten out a very difficult situation. Ultimately, failure to document your plans will leave your family less well-off than it might have been and greatly reduce your company's chances to prosper for another generation

CHAPTER 8

SELLING: THE ULTIMATE TRANSITION OPTION

For some reason many business owners adopt the attitude that anyone who sells a family-owned business is somehow admitting defeat. And, conversely, they consider the people who buy businesses to be aggressive, dominant players destined to control the rest of us. In fact I think it is impossible to state as a general rule whether sellers or buyers make out better in the long run. They just have different objectives or are at different points in their lives.

Of course in some instances business owners are forced to sell their companies under less-than-optimal circumstances. But these situations generally occur not because the buyers are aggressive businesspeople who can somehow take unfair advantage of the sellers. Typically business owners fail to sell their businesses in a financially successful way because they have failed to manage them effectively or to plan ahead for profitable transitions to retirement. In such cases owners who end up selling their companies in a "bad deal" may really be doing better than they would have done by continuing to lose money from a financially marginal operation. An owner who refuses to sell in such a situation because the prospective buyer is trying to "steal" the company may eventually have to liquidate the business in an even less profitable way.

In the opposite situation are business owners who have viable, growing companies with a strong positive cash flow. Business brokers, investment bankers, and other financial intermediaries have little trouble finding buyers for businesses like these as long as the sellers are willing to accept a reasonable price. If the intermediaries are doing their jobs well, prospective buyers often compete with one another and drive up the sales price. The sellers may walk away with small, or perhaps large, fortunes, and the buyers may later find it very difficult to recoup or make an adequate rate of return on their investments.

At any given time, assuming the local or national economy is not in a severe recession, there are always many more people who say they want to buy businesses than sell them. Many prospective buyers aren't really qualified, but then many prospective businesses available for sale are less-than-ideal candidates for an *INC.* magazine profile of a model company. If your business is earning an adequate return on investment as discussed in earlier chapters, you should be able—with reasonable planning, some common sense, and assistance from good legal, tax, and business advisors—to execute a sale of your company that meets your personal and financial needs. This can be a win-win situation for both you and the buyer. To the extent that the business you own is a desirable asset to other people, you are in a very strong position.

WHEN TO SELL

Most owners who intend to sell their businesses act on the assumption that the only logical time to sell is when they decide to retire. They apparently reason that, because they need a job of some sort until they retire, they must keep control of their businesses to ensure their own employment. Besides, they can sell their companies whenever they want to, right? And they think that the longer they keep their businesses the more they'll be worth.

Neither assumption is necessarily correct. Waiting until retirement or some other arbitrary target date to sell your business can in many situations be a bad decision. Depending on how specialized your business is or where it's located, you may not find very many potential buyers. You may have to be ready to sell your business at any time during a period of years and to move on a deal whenever a qualified buyer makes a reasonable offer. Failure to do so can mean waiting a very long time for another motivated buyer or taking a much lower price.

If you are familiar with the stock market, you know that making money in that type of investment requires not just knowing which stocks to buy but also making good decisions about when to sell. Investments that go up must, or at least can, come down. The same is true with the value of your business. In most cases the value of your company depends on the amount and growth rate of its earnings. Changes in industry profitability and market conditions over the years tend to result in lower earnings and growth. As a company grows older, it often becomes less profitable because the owner spends less time in the business or fails to keep up with new ideas and trends. If your business's value levels off or starts to decline, it may be better to go ahead and sell while it is at its peak value. This is one reason to have an independent appraiser keep you advised of your company's value and predict how it may be changing over time.

Another reason to remain open about the timing of your business sale is the ever-changing environment of income and estate taxes. Changes in the tax code enacted since 1986 have seriously decreased the after-tax dollars that many business owners will be able to receive from their companies. The most significant of these changes is the increase in the maximum capital gains tax rate from 20 percent to 28 percent. This change alone reduced most business owners' after-tax proceeds from the sale of their businesses by 10 percent. And since the beginning of 1989, corporations that sell their assets (except long-established S corporations) will be unable to escape corporate tax on the income from such a sale. Business owners who planned ahead and consulted their advisers could have saved a lot of tax expense by selling their businesses prior to these changes in the law. It is now necessary to plan the date of your potential business sale to take into account future changes in tax rates and other conditions that will affect your net proceeds from the sale.

In most situations the following set of conditions are ideal for choosing the right moment to sell your business.

1. Sales and profits show an upward trend. This condition helps to justify the highest earnings multiplier when a buyer values your business and sets a generally optimistic tone for the whole situation.
2. The management and employee team is complete. All the key people needed to run the business are in place, trained, and reasonably paid.
3. Industry and market trends are favorable. If most people agree that your industry or market has growth potential and your position in the market is strong, you will maximize value.

Obviously not all of these conditions exist all the time. In some cases the window of opportunity in terms of maximum value for your company may already have closed. The solution to this problem is to plan and think ahead about business conditions rather than react after the fact as many business owners do. If your company or market is at a cyclical peak and you want to get out of the business before another full business cycle can occur, then you had better sell now. Since, other things being equal, your company should command its maximum value when the conditions in the preceding list are present, you should really experience little lost income by selling early because you will receive a larger amount of money to reinvest in other assets.

A few years ago a business owner approached me for advice regarding the value of his company. The business on average had been highly successful. But it was in the cyclical building materials industry in a part of the country subject to extreme swings in its natural resource–dependent economy. After we had talked and I had studied his company and its market, I told him what I thought a fair price would be based on the company's earnings. Like many service-related businesses its value, based on earnings and cash flow at that time, was greater than the net worth of its assets. The owner was still a few years from a typical retirement age, but I advised him to consider selling immediately because the local economy was in a growth phase and his company was doing well by historical standards. His response was that he thought it would be foolish to sell while he was making so much money. But when he wanted to retire three years later, the economy in his market had declined dramatically. Potential local buyers who had been through other downturns could not afford his company. Out-of-staters were skeptical about getting involved in the economy. As a result, he couldn't find a qualified buyer at any reasonable price, so he'll be working a few years longer than he had planned.

GET READY TO SELL

Real estate agents typically advise property owners to spruce up their houses and get their ownership papers in order before attempting to sell their residences. That way the property will look its best for prospective buyers and the transaction will go smoothly. Doesn't it make sense to go through a similar but more complex preparation phase before attempting to sell a business?

People who may want to buy your company, not unlike your everyday customers, will usually be attracted or repelled by your business based on their initial impressions. Prospective buyers may be checking out your company and forming an opinion of its value even before you are ready to begin the selling process. So start getting your business into shape for sale now. It will take at least six months, and perhaps much longer, to carry out a complete inspection and correction program in all the areas outlined in this section. Even if you don't plan to sell your company soon, you will probably experience immediate benefits by carrying out these preparation steps because your business will simply function better and unwanted assets can be converted into cash.

Clean Up Your Act
Many private companies take on the appearance of an unkempt garage or basement. A junky, rundown appearance is a turnoff to prospective buyers, and it is also a turnoff to customers and employees. Budget some time and money to put your physical plant into presentable condition.

- Identify and correct all needed repairs, cleaning, and preventive maintenance in equipment and buildings.
- Repaint building exteriors, interiors, and signs.
- Get rid of or put in storage records and other paperwork and items not needed for day-to-day operations.
- Be sure that furniture and office decorations are appropriate and in good condition.
- Have appropriate, attractive, well-maintained landscaping.

Employee Appearance

Be sure that everyone in customer contact positions is greeting customers and conducting business in a courteous, professional manner. Some additional training and formulation of policies and standards can help in this regard. All employees should wear clothing or uniforms appropriate to their jobs and the image your company wants to portray. In most businesses prospective buyers will consider the quality and suitability of your employees to be at least as important as the quality and condition of your physical assets.

Asset Utilization and Efficiency

Companies tend to accumulate excess assets and marginal operations. These unneeded items tie up cash and reduce profitability. Getting rid of inefficient activities, obsolete assets, and unprofitable business units before the sale is the smart thing to do. The targets for much of the LBO and merger activity in the public stock market during the past few years have been companies whose assets were valued for less in the market than aggressive managers could earn by taking control and restructuring or revamping operations. Why sell your company to someone who will do that when with some effort you can capture the extra value yourself? It is all well and good to tell prospective buyers the things they can do to earn more cash than you have earned from your company. But they will virtually never pay you dollar for dollar for the opportunity to do so.

Get rid of unused equipment and excess inventory. Many business owners are reluctant to admit their mistakes and sell these items at a loss. But if you have unneeded assets that are worth less than you paid for them, you have already lost the money. Selling them causes you to recognize that loss, but at the same time it may provide some benefits. First, you will generate cash that can be invested elsewhere. You may be able to reduce operating costs by not renting as much space or by paying down debt and reducing interest expenses. And since your company's value is typically a multiple of earnings, you may more than recover your loss on the asset sale by the overall increase in your firm's value. Also, if your company is otherwise profitable, you will be able to recover some of these losses by reducing your income tax.

Prospective buyers for your entire company usually won't give you as much for some of your marginal assets as another buyer you locate yourself. A few years ago I bought an office computer that eventually became a real "Brand X" that virtually nobody knew anything about. It had almost no general market value. Yet I discovered by checking around carefully that other businesses had substantial investments in that same brand of computer and were still relying on it for office automation. Those companies were thrilled to find a good used model that was compatible with their software and their employees' training, and they were willing to pay top dollar.

A similar dilemma confronted one of my clients who had some obsolete machine tools that had taken up space for years. The equipment's value as junk was nothing because it would be so expensive to move. Although the tools could no longer produce competitive work in my client's industry, they turned out to be useful for in-house maintenance work at another company. Not only was the other company willing to pay several thousand dollars for the "obsolete" equipment, but they moved them away in their own trucks with their own labor. The proceeds from the sale could be profitably reinvested and the room that the obsolete tools had occupied was rented to another business for storage space. How many profitable clean-up projects are lurking around your company?

Besides inventory and fixed assets, many businesses have too much money tied up in accounts receivable. Again, prospective business buyers will probably give you little or nothing for old receivables. If you have truly bad receivables, you might as well face the fact and at least take a tax deduction if possible. Perhaps your delinquent customers value their credit rating but just can't pay the entire amount. Why not offer them a discount? Anything you receive is better than nothing, and they may pay you a discounted amount before they pay other creditors. Your bad receivables will come to light during an astute buyer's investigation, and the buyer may not give you any credit for the bad receivables. Even worse, your bad receivables will reflect poorly on your company's profitability record because an analyst might conclude that you overstated past sales and earnings. Furthermore, the value of your customer base and employees' abilities will be questioned.

If you have property, equipment, or parts of your business operations that you want to keep after the sale of your main business, identify them and separate them clearly in your financial records. Provided there are no negative tax consequences, you may want to spin these assets off into separate companies or partnerships that you will continue to own. These separate entities can even lease assets back or provide services to your original company. Ideally you should think about these things early on and set up separate entities for the various assets so that you can avoid double taxation when you sell your company.

Get Your Financial Homework Done
All your financial records should be up-to-date, complete, and accurate. These provide the evidence you need to back up all the favorable words and feelings you have about your business. You can talk all you want about reputation, goodwill, and so forth, but if you don't have believable numbers to back up your story, you won't get the best price for your business. Income statements and balance sheets prepared in a consistent manner and preferably in accordance with accepted accounting principles should be available for at least the last three to five years. If your business is cyclical, then you may need information over a longer period.

Your income statements should separate sales by product or service. It may also be useful to have records of the number of units of various products sold or the relative amount sold in different locations or market segments for each time period so that buyers can tell which parts of your business are expanding or contracting. Ideally this information should show that the most profitable products or locations are expanding and therefore indicate that your business will be more valuable in the future. Expense items should be easily identifiable as fixed or variable costs. The buyer should be able to understand which production costs are associated with various products, jobs, or locations. One-time expenses or income and all forms of compensation to the owners should be itemized and explained.

If your balance sheets are made in accordance with general accounting principles, they may value some of your assets at substantially lower than their market value. Typical assets in this category are real estate and equipment that has been subjected to accelerated depreciation. If you have such assets, prepare an additional *adjusted* balance sheet showing the actual value of each asset. Be prepared with evidence such as appraisals, tax assessments, or other documentation to support your value adjustments.

If you prepare complete financial statements only once or twice a year, at least compile monthly or quarterly revenue figures. You probably have to provide these already for state or local taxes. They will be useful for demonstrating the current trends in your business's most important financial variable. You will also need to come up with current calculations for inventory, receivables, and payables so that general profitability since the last financial statement can be estimated. And if you expect the buyer to assume any long-term debts, you should compile the current balances and payment schedule for those debts along with copies of the notes themselves.

Finally, if you are selling the stock of a corporation, the buyer will want to have copies of all the relevant tax returns and other tax-filing documents. It will be important to prove that you are in compliance with all tax laws, since whoever buys the stock of a company will be buying any contingent liabilities for unpaid or underpaid taxes. Depending on your business you may also need to provide assurances regarding such things as toxic wastes, safety, and environmental regulations and employment laws.

Corporate or Other Business Records

After initially filing for incorporation many small businesses fail to meet the letter of their state's corporation laws. Annual meetings and board resolutions are frequently undocumented, and stock ownership records may be incomplete. If you are planning to sell the corporation or any of its major assets, you must work with your attorney to be sure you are in compliance with all applicable laws. Failure to do so can slow down your sale negotiations and even lead to the invalidation of a sale after the fact.

Your company may have contractual agreements such as leases, supplier contracts, franchises, licenses, or customer contracts. Pull together all these documents. Review them to make certain they are current and in order. Also, many franchise agreements, distribution agreements, and licenses give another party a degree of control over how and to whom you can sell your business. If there are any such constraints on the sale of your business, be sure to clarify and confidentially discuss your intent to sell the business with those third parties so they do not raise objections when you are trying to consummate a deal. Find out exactly how a prospective buyer will be able to qualify to take over your franchise or product line. If your work force is unionized, then you may also need to ensure that your labor contract is up-to-date and in compliance.

Employment Policies and Procedures

Make sure that vacation, sick leave, working conditions, and other important employee policies are documented and enforced. This will give prospective buyers confidence that your employees are used to working under conditions that are normal for your industry or similar kinds of companies. You should be able to demonstrate from your records that your business is in compliance with applicable labor laws and that all your potential liabilities for vacation time, payroll taxes, and so forth are fully accounted for in your financial records.

DECIDE WHAT YOUR POSTSALE INVOLVEMENT WILL BE

As you prepare to sell your business, be sure to think through what your involvement, if any, will be after you sell. It is important to let prospective buyers know this early on because it will affect their decision about whether they want to buy the company and how much they are willing to pay. Your basic decision is whether you want to stay on with your company after it is sold or to remove yourself from the operations as soon as possible. In most cases you will have to be available for a while after the sale to help the new owner become familiar with employees, customers, suppliers, and operations. This is usually specified in the sales agreement. Typically a time limit is set on such involvement, and your compensation may or may not be separate from the overall sale price.

If you want to remove yourself from the business as soon as possible after a sale, you will have to make an extra effort to be sure everything in your company is well-organized and documented for the new owner. After that, if you have sold wisely, you will be able to relax and collect income from your sale proceeds.

In many cases the buyer may want you to stay with the company in a management or technical capacity. If you agree to this, then you will typically receive compensation for these services in addition to payment for the value of the business. Sometimes buyers will give the former owners a higher price, called an *earn out*, for the company if it achieves certain sales and earnings targets after the ownership change is complete. If you honestly believe that your business has more profit potential than its history demonstrates and you are able to deliver on that belief with the additional capital or other resources provided by the purchaser, then this can be a very lucrative arrangement for you.

IDENTIFY THE PROSPECTIVE BUYERS

Who on earth wants to buy your business? Some business owners will have lots of potential buyers to choose from, and some will have few. The number of prospective buyers your business attracts largely depends on how desirable it is in terms of earnings record, market potential, and manageability. Although there are generally more prospective business buyers than sellers, this is not necessarily the case for your company.

If things are going poorly with your company, then perhaps nobody really wants to buy it. I have seen the sad situation in which the owners of a long-established company failed to control costs and make adjustments when many of their customers fell on hard times and reduced their purchases. The once highly profitable company had been allowed to deteriorate into a serious turnaround situation. Because several parties had approached the owners over the years to inquire about buying the company, everyone was confident they could easily find a buyer. But despite the fact that the company was a representative for several important national brands and had a good reputation among its customers, nobody was interested in buying under any terms. With their bank putting on pressure, the owners' only option was a liquidation sale at auction prices.

Most businesses that are presently or potentially profitable and are not overly dependent on the specific abilities of the current owner/manager can generally be sold given sufficient time and a reasonable marketing effort. Start by being open-minded about prospective buyers, and make a list of all the likely prospects.

Larger Companies

Your business may be a candidate for acquisition by a much larger company. Many small companies have unique products, techniques, or locations that are difficult for larger companies to duplicate. From the large companies' perspective, purchasing a small business may be the result of a *make-buy* decision. That is, the larger company may have decided that it's cheaper to buy an existing small company that can be expanded to a larger scale than to make a particular product or enter a new market from scratch. Even though it may cost more initially to buy an existing company, the price can often be recovered by entering the market more quickly and having immediate cash flow from existing operations. Sometimes a national or regional company looks at purchasing a small local firm in its industry as the equivalent of opening a branch operation without the need to incur start-up losses.

Keep track of what is being published about the plans of larger companies in your industry. If they are purchasing companies like yours, information about the deals will be reported to the Securities and Exchange Commission if they are public companies and in the trade press if they aren't.

Suppliers

Companies that provide you with materials and services may be interested in buying your business. If you are an important customer, your suppliers may be afraid of losing your account to a competitor if someone else buys your company. In other words, suppliers may be looking not only to buy the revenue and earnings from your operations but also to lock in the profits they make on their sales to you. Therefore, they may be willing to pay a premium price.

Also your suppliers may want to become more vertically integrated in the industry. By integrating *downstream*, they gain the ability to expand the sale of products and possibly move into new business opportunities. If this is their strategy, the best way to carry it out would be to purchase their own customers' businesses since it would be costly and difficult to compete with their own outlets.

Customers

One or more of your commercial customers may want to vertically integrate *upstream* to control their own sources of supply. This is particularly true if these customers add value to your product or service as part of their production process. By purchasing their source of supply for a major input, your customers have the chance to gain additional profit margin and ensure a reliable source of materials or other inputs.

Competitors

In some ways competitors are the trickiest potential buyer group to deal with, but I think that many people overestimate the difficulty of doing so. Business owners assume that in a sale they will automatically have to deal with competitors from a position of weakness. But this is only true if their companies are in a difficult financial situation or have few prospective buyers. And in that case they will be in a difficult situation no matter whom they are dealing with.

The truth is that if your company is a viable force in its market, your competitors may have the most to gain as buyers and may therefore be willing to pay the highest price. More companies commonly compete in a given market than can really make a good profit. Buying a competitor and absorbing its sales without taking on additional overhead expense can be a profitable strategy. Buying "used" production capacity or sales outlets is usually much less expensive than building new ones.

One day a client mentioned that one of her weaker competitors was having a hard time and wanted to sell his business. She had rejected the possibility of buying his company because she thought the asking price was laughable given that his business was unprofitable and always had been. But the seller was very stubborn and insisted that the price could not be reduced because he wanted to recover what he calculated to be his investment. Technically my client was correct. The asking price was theoretically too high. But it was not much higher than the cost of an equivalent amount of new production capacity. And the incremental sales increase, after cutting out the competitor's administration and marketing costs, would be highly profitable to my client. Also, if a large company bought out her competitor and invested a lot of money in the operation, it might drive her into an unprofitable position. When we had evaluated all the facts, it looked as if the seller's asking price wasn't such a bad deal after all, and my client purchased the company. Two years later this has turned out to be a good deal because with a beefed-up marketing program my client needs all the merchandise she can produce, and it is much more difficult for anyone to enter her market. The high initial price turned out to be a win-win deal after all. Maybe some of your competitors can be convinced of the same thing.

You take some obvious risks when you approach competitors with a sales proposal. First, you have to be careful about showing them cost and customer information that may give them a competitive advantage against you if the deal doesn't go through. But you can protect yourself to a certain extent with strong nondisclosure and noncompete agreements regarding the information you show them. Also, rather than become serious buyers, your competitors may take your approach as a signal to go all out to capture market share knowing that you may be reluctant to invest heavily just before selling your company.

Managers and Employees

Managers and employees obviously know your business and are interested in its future. In some cases they are logical buyers if for no other reason than they are "suppliers" to your business and will want to prevent an outside buyer from coming in and replacing them. If you don't plan to leave your business to your family, selling it to employees may seem like the next best thing to do. You may see it as a means to reward people who have worked to help build your business.

Two problems are commonly associated with selling a company to managers or employees. The smallest private companies seldom have enough strong managers with the ability and vision to run the entire business successfully. Many people who are loyal and competent staff members are really incapable of being leaders. This problem can be solved by spending more time and effort in locating and developing possible successor management. You may want to bring in a potential CEO as a middle manager to get to know your business while you get to know her or him. Such a move may more than pay for itself by bringing new skills, ideas, and energy into your business. If you pay the new person in part with performance bonuses and stock options, he or she will begin developing a commitment to ownership, and you will be developing a buyer.

Even if you think your managers and employees are well-qualified to run your company, in many cases they are not qualified buyers. That is, they don't have enough money to buy your company. Depending on the nature of your assets and the financial strength of your operations, your employees may be able to arrange financing from commercial sources. But if they cannot, then you may have to finance the sale yourself. And if your employees cannot come up with a large down payment, you may have to take your payment in a risky long-term note.

One interesting option for selling all or part of your company to employees is an employee stock ownership plan (ESOP). Because the federal government has decided to encourage employee ownership, such a plan has some major incentives:

1. The money (both interest and principal) your company spends to buy ESOP stock is tax deductible to your company because it is considered a contribution to an employee benefit plan.
2. If your company qualifies for a loan to buy ESOP stock, banks will usually charge a lower interest rate because part of their income from interest earned on an ESOP loan is tax-free.
3. Since you are selling stock to the ESOP, you will likely receive the most favorable tax treatment currently available. And if you sell 30 percent or more of your stock to an ESOP, you may be able to defer a substantial portion of your taxes on proceeds you put into certain qualified investments.

These incentives are not the only benefits of an ESOP. Employees who perceive themselves as owners may be more productive, although this point is far from proven. An ESOP program that is implemented over a number of years can be part of a long-term process of developing internal management resources to run the business after you withdraw. And once you sell part of your ownership to an ESOP and invest the proceeds elsewhere, your diversified investment portfolio will reduce part of the typical financial risk associated with owning a small company.

If you continue to work for your company while you are selling stock to the ESOP, you will end up getting part of your stock back as an employee benefit. You can then sell it to the company again, just like other employees, in accordance with your plan provisions. That's really having your cake and eating it too!

ESOPs can, however, be fairly expensive and complex to set up and maintain. The value of stock contributed to the ESOP will have to be determined and documented by a third party in compliance with IRS guidelines, and the valuation will have to be updated annually. If you are selling minority ownership positions to the ESOP, the value placed on that stock according to IRS guidelines may not be as much as you feel you could get if you sold the whole company on the open market. You'll have to determine whether the reduction in value, if any, is offset by the tax and other advantages of the ESOP.

Also, some employees expect that as ESOP participants they will suddenly have more control over day-to-day decisions. In some cases this is true. But in many cases it is not, and then some employees become disgruntled. The truth is that many times it is no more practical for employees to have control in a small ESOP company than for employees who are also minority stockholders to have control in a large public company.

Business Associates

If none of your suppliers, customers, or competitors wants to buy your business, then one of their employees just might. It is quite common for the sales representative of a large company to purchase one of the businesses he or she has sold products to over the years. Sometimes, too, a customer's key employee may buy a supplier's business because his or her company offers a limited future. These people may know your business well and if they do not burn bridges with their former employers may even be able to strike better supplier or customer agreements than you can. Likewise, the frustrated employee of a competitor may be champing at the bit to run his or her own show and may be able to transfer some accounts and personal goodwill into your business after taking it over.

Sometimes your lawyer, accountant, or other professional advisers are possible buyers. Like other people they may want to make career changes and become independent business owners. Although they may not have hands-on experience with your company, they frequently have a thorough knowledge of many aspects of the business and can be fast learners.

Miscellaneous Third Parties

Despite the potential of buyers like those already listed, you may in fact end up selling your business to someone who has no prior connection to either you or the company. Such buyers may be employees from other companies looking for career changes, independent investors, or frustrated would-be entrepreneurs who are not prepared to start their own companies from scratch. These are the people who typically make the rounds of business brokers, investment bankers, CPAs, commercial bankers, consultants, and other potential intermediaries hoping to be referred to prospective sellers. Sometimes these people are qualified buyers in terms of financial resources as well as experience and skills. But more often they are hopeful tire-kickers looking for a "steal" or simply trying to find a business owner desperate enough to sell for easy terms with nothing down. If for any reason your business is not highly desirable, you will probably have to deal with this kind of buyer. Sometimes this situation can turn into a good deal for everyone involved, especially if both sides do their homework and don't make unwarranted assumptions about the deal.

But many times these sales turn into nightmares when a naive buyer bites off too much in terms of either financial or management requirements. Such a transaction then becomes highly risky to you as a seller because you will probably have to finance a good portion of the transaction. You may end up getting your business back with fewer assets and a more tarnished image than when you initially sold it.

DECIDING WHOM TO APPROACH

Once you have listed all the prospective buyers available to you in the categories just discussed, you will have a good starting point for finding the right buyer for your business. You can probably narrow your search to relatively few candidates by looking at your business from each potential buyer's perspective and estimating who is most likely to agree with you about the price, terms, and conditions you want.

If one of your most important requirements is to remove yourself completely from business operations as soon as possible after the sale, then you will need to approach the sellers who are best able to get along without your help. These may be current employees or the employees of other companies in your industry who will know as much as you do. On the other hand, if you want to sell your company but remain active as a manager, you may want to focus on larger companies, suppliers, and customers. Those buyers will probably want to staff your company with a professional manager, as opposed to an owner/manager, and would therefore be open to keeping you in place after the sale or bringing you into their own management group.

If you want to be completely cashed out at the date of sale rather than take a contract for part of the value, then you will need to approach the buyers who have the deepest pockets. Despite wishful thinking few companies can be purchased with little or no money down unless the seller is willing to finance part of the deal. And most banks or other financial sources will still require the buyers to put a certain amount of equity into the deal. If you have any doubt about a prospective buyer's financial resources, you should obtain evidence of financial qualification early on in the process. As a client who was looking for someone to purchase his highly successful company once said to me, "I don't want to sell this business to anyone who doesn't have a lot more money than I did when I bought it."

Selling to a cash buyer obviously reduces your risk, but cash buyers may not always be willing to pay top dollar. If your goal is to obtain the maximum price for your company, then you have to approach the buyers who think they can make the most money from your business. In many cases these will be suppliers or competitors. Unless your current suppliers are the only source for your products, they will always be concerned about losing your account if your business changes hands or if the new owner does not operate it well. Therefore, even a supplier who doesn't want to buy your company may be willing to help locate and even provide financial support to a trustworthy buyer. This situation can help you obtain both a high price and good terms.

A competitor who wants to prevent you from selling to someone else who will be strongly competitive may also be willing to pay a high price. Your competitor can justify this move by the *synergies* that the acquisition will create. By estimating which of your overhead expenses your competitor can eliminate without harming sales and earnings, you can estimate how much more the business is worth to your competitor than to another buyer. For example, suppose you have determined that your company is worth six times annual pretax earnings. To a competitor who could eliminate $50,000 in administration and accounting expenses, your company should be worth $300,000 more than it would be worth to another buyer. You may not be able to bargain for all of this premium, but you should be able to capture some of it.

Some business owners are concerned about how their employees will be treated after the sale. They are afraid that a new owner will "clean house" and eliminate some jobs or reduce salaries after the purchase, and they don't want to throw long-time employees/friends to the wolves. I have seen several situations in which sellers, out of a sense of obligation, want to restrict buyers' treatment of certain employees. You must face the fact that if some of your employees are overpaid or under-productive, then new owners will naturally want to remove them in order to realize the earnings necessary to justify the price they paid for your business. If you want to protect such employees' incomes, then the value of your business will be reduced.

USE PROFESSIONAL ADVISERS

Selling even a small business is a complex task that you may do only once in your life. To increase the odds of maximizing your income from the transaction and avoiding serious errors in judgment, you should use qualified professional advisers from the very beginning of the process. Good advice is expensive, but the cost of errors is even more expensive. If attorneys, CPAs, consultants, and intermediaries did not consistently provide their clients with information and services worth at least as much as they charge for them, then they would soon be out of business themselves. In fact these professions are flourishing because the business environment even for the smallest companies has become highly complex and sophisticated. The best approach is to put together a team of advisers, inform them of your intention and timetable for selling, and ask them to help you address these topics:

1. Are your business's legal records, stockholder agreements, tax obligations, contractual obligations, etc., in order? Your attorney and CPA should report on this.
2. What methods of sale are appropriate in your situation, and what are the tax and other consequences of each option? Your attorney and CPA can recommend methods that will have the greatest net benefit for you.
3. How much is your business worth, and what steps might you take to increase its value? A business valuation specialist, investment banker, or experienced business broker can help with this. You may want to get more than one opinion.
4. Who are the likely buyers? You can come up with ideas by considering the list of potential buyers discussed previously. Your advisory team may come up with more names. If you don't know many qualified buyers, then you should consult an investment banker or business broker.
5. What information will be provided to prospective buyers? A one-page description of your business along with the asking price and terms should be written. This need not identify your company and may be given to buyers to determine initial interest. A more complete prospectus with detailed information and several years' financial statements should be prepared in advance to show to serious buyers.
6. Who will deal directly with the buyers? This may be an investment banker or broker. It might also be your attorney, CPA, or other knowledgeable person whose judgment you trust.
7. Who will wrap up the paperwork once a deal is struck? Normally your attorney and CPA will handle this.

WHAT ABOUT FINANCIAL INTERMEDIARIES?

Many times the most desirable private companies are marketed without financial intermediaries. That is because the company is sold to one of the "related parties" described in the previous section and never really goes on the open market. Such a closed sale offers some potential advantages. First, you can avoid paying an intermediary's commission, which would be quite high for a small company. Typically, intermediaries charge 5 to 7 percent for businesses worth less than $500,000 and drop about 1 percent for each additional $500,000 of value. The commission on a $2 million sale would amount to $70,000 to $100,000, not an inconsequential amount.

In addition, by dealing with known, identified buyers, you can usually maintain the desired level of confidentiality and keep the process well-controlled. The greater level of confidence associated with familiar buyers eliminates the stress involved in opening your business to the tire-kickers or unqualified buyers who might be brought in by a broker.

On the other hand, a good investment banker or broker will have contacts with qualified potential buyers well beyond the circle known to you and your other advisers. Although their fees are high, such intermediaries can more than pay for themselves by helping to get maximum value for your company. They also have an incentive to help complete the deal in a timely manner, which, if done properly, should be to your advantage as well. Finally the intermediaries should be able to keep the transactions on an impartial professional level that is very difficult for the sellers themselves to maintain.

Intermediaries may, however, try to convince you to accept a poor or marginal deal because from their point of view any deal is better than no deal. You can guard against that by setting specific standards for the intermediary's performance. You may want to engage a secondary adviser whose compensation does not depend on the deal's going through.

Be sure that you interview several potential intermediaries and check their references carefully. It is vital that you have good rapport with and complete confidence in whomever you engage for this important transaction.

YOU NAME THE PRICE AND I'LL NAME THE TERMS

Once you've found a suitable buyer for your company and had a general meeting of the minds regarding your company's value, your final hurdle will be the terms of sale. If the business world were a simple place, then business sales would always be cash transactions. But in reality sales of private companies are typically not straightforward, all-cash transactions. This is usually the result of some variation on these circumstances:

1. The buyer is a public company and wants to pay for the transaction with stock.
2. The buyer and seller cannot agree on the precise value, so the buyer wants part of the price contingent on future performance.
3. Part of the sales price is in the form of an employment, noncompete, or consulting agreement.
4. The buyer cannot raise all the purchase price, so the seller has to finance part of the deal.

Given that most of the people who want to buy your business will be neither willing nor able to pay the entire purchase price in cash, you should think ahead about the type of terms that are acceptable. You can reduce the part of your company's value that the buyer has to finance in several ways. Driving too hard a bargain on both price and terms can be harmful to you in the long run if the buyer can't meet the terms of sale and you get the business back in your lap. Not only will you have to go through the long process of selling your company again, but the business you get back may be less valuable than the one you sold after the buyer had to cut corners to try to keep up with the payments to you.

The prospective buyer of your business may offer to exchange stock in his or her company for the stock of your company. The offer may be for all stock, or it may be for part cash and part stock. This method of payment presents some possible advantages and disadvantages for the seller. By exchanging the stock of your company for the stock of another company, you will be able to defer paying income tax on your gain from the sale until you eventually sell the stock you received. You may be able to arrange for all or part of this stock to pass into your estate without ever paying income tax. This tax deferment lets you effectively reinvest your pretax proceeds from the sale and allow those proceeds to multiply until you are ready to sell the stock. It also lets you control the timing of your tax payments by choosing when to sell the stock you receive. The best possible advantage of a stock exchange is also the greatest potential disadvantage. If the stock of the acquiring company increases in value, then the amount you receive for your company will increase as well. It is possible to hitch yourself to a rising star and do very well. On the other hand, if the stock you receive declines in value, it could have a dramatic negative effect on the value you ultimately receive from the sale. The potential for a downside disaster can be partly mitigated by receiving a portion of sales price in cash and insisting on a higher price for accepting stock than you would have required for an all-cash deal.

When you place a value on your company, you will typically view its prospects from the most optimistic point of view, but the buyer will naturally tend to be more pessimistic. Therefore you and the buyer may not be able to agree. Assuming that both parties are dealing in good faith, however, you should be able to arrange for the eventual price, above a certain minimum fixed amount, to be contingent on actual future business performance. If handled well, this can be a kind of guarantee for the buyer and provide a chance for the seller to participate in the future growth of the company. The success of such an arrangement requires several elements.

The seller and buyer need to be able to identify exactly why they differ in their perception of the business's value. One typical source of disagreement arises when the seller puts a greater value on the business because for one reason or another he or she believes it is poised for a virtually automatic increase in sales that will allow it to earn more in the future than it has earned in the past. Or maybe the buyer feels that the price of a key expense item will increase uncontrollably in the future, and therefore, all other things being equal, the business will earn less than the seller contends. Once the basic cause of the difference in value perception has been identified, you can devise a formula that satisfies both sides: the buyer agrees to pay the seller a royalty or bonus in the event the business does as well as the seller claims it will, but the buyer pays only the base price if the business does not perform well.

As a buyer you should be leery of linking the contingent part of your payment to something as nebulous as profit. Instead, you should make sure your contingent payment is based on a specifically identified variable that is not easily manipulated by changes in accounting methods. The performance variable that is the easiest to keep track of is the *top line*, or sales. The one that is most subject to manipulation and vagueness is the *bottom line*, or net income.

A client of mine had never really made any money in his business, and sales had been declining. But he had reason to believe that a particular buyer would be able to increase revenues substantially and therefore make a large profit because most of the business's costs were fixed. Because the business had not been profitable, however, the buyer only wanted to pay for the value of the relatively meager fixed assets. Also, he wanted the seller to provide relatively easy financing terms. As a compromise we insisted that if annual sales increased to a level greater than they had been in prior years, then in addition to the set payments for the portion of the fixed assets that the seller had financed the buyer would pay a royalty of 5 percent of all sales above the level of the company's best prior year. This arrangement was fair to the seller because, if the business did not have the growth potential he claimed, then it was probably not even worth the cost of the assets. The result was that the new owner did experience a dramatic sales increase, and therefore the seller received a royalty that greatly increased his total proceeds from the sale. Although the buyer moaned about having to pay more for the business than he had originally planned, it really wasn't a bad deal because (1) the seller was correct about the earnings potential of the business, (2) the buyer was able to finance the fixed assets at favorable terms, and (3) unlike the payment for the business, the royalty payments are immediately and fully tax-deductible to the buyer.

Under many circumstances the party that buys a business will want to have part of the consideration paid in the form of employment, noncompetition, or consulting agreements. In some cases the buyer of your business may really need your continuing involvement in the company, and you may want to continue working. If so, the payment for your employment or consulting should be in addition to the value of your business. In other cases the buyer might simply want to pay you or some of your key employees not to use your expertise and contacts to compete and take sales away from your original company. An agreement not to compete may therefore increase your business's value. There are several advantages to these agreements. The ability to spread the proceeds from the sale over several years may give the seller some tax advantages. Also, if you agree to accept compensation from these contracts, you may be able to increase the effective selling price of your company because, under a reasonable agreement, the buyer may be able to deduct the payments from the business's taxable income. If you remain an employee of your company, you might also be able to remain in the group medical plan, pension plan, or other benefit programs that would cost you a lot more money to duplicate on your own

The most common reason that sellers don't receive all cash for their businesses is that the buyers willing to pay the most money, or sometimes the only potential buyers, cannot come up with enough cash to swing the deal. Be wary of the first type of buyer. Someone who offers a higher nominal price for your business but insists on easy terms may only *seem* to be paying the price you want. If the interest rate being offered on the note is less than you can earn on alternative investments, then you are effectively giving the buyer a discount. And taking a contract in payment for your former business, which will be operated without your day-to-day control and subject to various economic risks, is probably a much greater risk than most alternative investments. There are several ways to reduce your risk when selling your business on a contract.

Take as much value as possible out of your business before the sale. This means that inventories, receivables, and any other feasible assets should be converted to cash and distributed out of the company. You may have to do this over a period of time before the business is sold. Since there are not presently any favorable capital gains tax rates for sale of businesses, this strategy may involve no negative tax effect.

You may also be able to reduce risk by diversifying the sale of your business's assets. If you own property in which the business operates, you may want to sell the property to someone other than the buyer of the business. Besides reducing the risk that the business buyer may default on both the property and the business, you may increase the universe of potential buyers for both assets and receive a higher total price. Owning real estate and other fixed assets is typically considered a lower-risk investment than owning the small business that occupies that real estate or uses those assets. Therefore your business's value may be maximized by selling or financing the fixed assets separately from your operating business. For example, as shown in Table 8–1, your business may be earning a pretax income of $140,000 and occupy property that you own and therefore pay no rent to use. If a buyer thinks that the business, including the property, is worth seven times pretax income, then the total value of the assets would be about $1 million. But suppose the business signed a lease requiring it to pay $40,000 per year in rent for use of the property. This would make the pretax business income $100,000, and the operating business would be worth about $700,000. Therefore you could sell the business but keep the property and receive rent payments while, with luck, the property appreciates. Or if the rent is at market rate, you could sell the property to another investor. Since real estate typically sells for a higher multiple of its income than does a closely held business, the total value of your assets may be maximized by selling them separately.

Not only may separating your assets for sale result in a greater potential value, but the risk may be reduced as well. Assuming the prospective buyer has a fixed amount of money available for a down payment, the fewer assets you sell, the larger the down payment will be as a percentage of the amount financed. This reduces the amount of money you are owed in

TABLE 8–1
Selling Business and Property: Package Deal
versus Separate Sale

A. Value of Business and Property as a Package

Annual pretax earnings	$140,000
Pretax earnings multiplier	× 7
Imputed business value	$980,000

B. Value of Business and Property Sold Separately

Net market rate rent for property	$ 40,000
Pretax earnings multiplier for property	× 10
Imputed property value	$ 400,000
Annual pretax earnings after rent payment	$ 100,000
Pretax earnings multiplier	× 7
Imputed business value	$ 700,000
Total value of business plus property	$1,100,000

the event of a default. It also reduces the chance of default itself because the buyer will have smaller payments to make.

Under the current tax code this concept of separate sale of assets will be feasible only if the seller has had the foresight to own the salable fixed assets separately from the other business assets or to conduct business as a partnership or S corporation. Otherwise, owning all the assets in a standard corporation may create a double-taxation problem.

Steps that will increase the value or reduce the risk of selling your company on a contract include

1. Obtaining the largest possible down payment.
2. Having a security interest in the business assets you have sold. You should also retain voting control on major decisions involving additional debt, the sale of significant assets, and salaries or dividends until the debts to you are paid.
3. Requiring the company to maintain specific financial ratios for such things as debt-to-equity, current-assets-to-current-liabilities, or income-to-debt service.

4. Charging a rate of interest that covers the risk of your investment and fluctuates up or down with changing market conditions.
5. Obtaining the buyer's personal guarantee, secured by his or her personal assets.

A Foolproof Formula for a Disastrous Experience in Selling Your Business

Don't even think about selling your business until poor health, advanced age, impending death, or catastrophe makes it inevitable.

Let your business deteriorate from its prime operating condition to a level just short of financial distress.

Make sure that your financial records are incomplete and/or out of date.

Keep your plans a complete secret from your attorney, CPA, and other advisers. Go to them only at the last minute when it is too late to change any details of the transaction.

If you use a broker, make sure it is someone who contacted you at random looking for cold leads. Don't check any references or qualifications.

Even if you use intermediaries and independent advisers, insist on dealing personally with the prospective buyer. This will introduce the maximum emotion and stress into the situation.

After everything is complete and nothing can be changed, bring in an experienced professional to second-guess the deal so you will know how badly you really did.

INDEX

Financial intermediaries,
158–59
Financial leverage, 95, 97
Financial statements, 62–66,
144–46
Free cash, 58, 95
Free cash flow, 59, 66, 72
Freezing an estate, 127, 129

G

General Utilities Doctrine,
15, 103
Gifts, 127, 129
Going concern value, 76
Goodwill, 76–77, 144
Gross margin, 100
Gross profit, 37, 100
Growth phase, 34–35

H

Highly profitable businesses, 43
Historical earnings assumption,
81
Holding company, 50–51, 85–86

I

Income statement, 63, 144–45
Income tax, 6, 12, 103, 143
Inflation, 14, 36, 50, 73, 132
Initial investment, 2–3, 5, 6–14
Intangible value, 76
Inventory levels, 39, 163
Investment recovery, 3–4
Investors' returns, 46–49

L

Levers, 92

M

Make-buy decision, 148
Managers and employees (as
buyers), 151–53
Marketing strategy, 23
Market saturation, 20
Maturity phase, 23, 35–36
Maximizing earnings, 13–14
Mergers and acquisitions,
77, 142
Mom-and-Pop businesses,
80

N

Negative cash flow, 23, 24,
30, 34, 91
Noncompetition agreements,
159, 162
Nonfamily managers, 134–35
Normally profitable businesses,
43
Normal working hours, 105

O

Operating company, 49–50,
85–86
Opportunity cost, 5–6, 11,
13, 34, 42, 63, 68
Ordinary income, 49
Overhead, 3, 88, 150
Owners' discretionary cash
flow, 87
Ownership
changing, 111
and the decision-making
process, 132–33
defined, 108
determining the structure,
109–11